Freedom Talks
No. II

by

Julia Seton

Freedom Talks
No. II
by Julia Seton

Copyright © 2023

All Rights reserved.

ISBN: 978-93-59394-37-4

Published by

DOUBLE 9 BOOKS

2/13-B, Ansari Road
Daryaganj, New Delhi – 110002
info@double9books.com
www.double9books.com
Tel. 011-40042856

ABOUT THE AUTHOR

Freedom Talks No. II was written by Julia Seton, a well-known author whose work has left a lasting mark on the literary world. Seton's words have an unmatched ability to inspire and free people because she has a deep knowledge of how people work and is always looking for the truth. Seton has spent her long and successful career trying to figure out what makes people tick, throwing light on the things that get in the way of personal growth and self-realization. Her unique point of view goes against social rules and makes people question the limits that are put on them. Seton is a visionary in her own right. She explores the depths of awareness without fear, weaving together captivating stories and deep insights that touch readers' souls. Her work is like a guiding light that shows the way to freedom and self-empowerment.

CONTENTS

The Secret Of Healing

"In the beginning was the word, and the word was with God and the word was God."

"And the word was made flesh and dwelt among us, and we beheld his glory full of grace and truth."

Ever since the birth of the human race there have been health and disease. Everywhere we find those who live at levels of comprehension that cannot express in flesh the perfect power of the word and these must by natural law take on the form of whatever they have power to comprehend.

Health is man's immortal birthright; it is eternal in the universal plan, and it can be made to become eternal in the life of men in just the hour they understand the laws of their own being.

There are two expressions of energy in the universe; one is called the constructive, the other the destructive; the one builds up, the other tears down. This must forever be so, for only as matter is destroyed and passed back into energy can the energy pass out again into finer forms.

Living in these great universal currents of construction and destruction, man relates himself constantly with one or both through the simple law of his own consciousness, and only as he learns the laws of his own being and consciously places himself in a position of power can he ever hope to escape the results which the negative, destructive currents produce in his body and his environment.

Today we know that the world in which we live is nothing but a great sea of energy which, in the undifferentiated, is called God, and in the differentiated is called matter or form, or, to make it more simple, we can call one the energy that creates, and the other the things created from and by this energy.

Man and his environment are created by this energy: He is a localized center of force and he becomes the expression in form of just whatever he relates with under the law of cosmic correspondence.

We have found that this great energy is also *intelligence* and is nothing but mind with its various manifestations. We know today that the atoms of the atmosphere are intelligence, and as they touch one another throughout space, it is through this atomic mind that messages are carried, and currents are generated which can heal patients at a distance.

Everything in the universe is in a state of intelligent association, and when the atoms become expressed in human form, they pass into that expression of the universal mind known as *human* consciousness.

All human life is simply different tastes of consciousness brought about by the different vibratory rates to which our atoms respond.

The physical body is composed of a group of atoms attuned to move at a certain vibratory rate, and within this physical body is another body of finer atoms attuned to a still higher vibration and in relationship with the higher electrical currents of the universe. There has not been much told about this finer body, but it is time the sick world knows this law of being, for then it will be in a position to control its own life. This finer body is the "thought body" or psychic body and it is upon this that the physical body depends for its power, just as the very best instrument in the world depends upon the player for its expressed melody.

All sight, all hearing, all function is in this psychic body, not in the physical one. What many of the psychologists call the subconscious mind is only the registered intelligence of the psychic self. This psychic self is in direct communication with the cosmic self and with the physical self, and it is through this we become cosmic in our human consciousness.

The psychic body manifests through *idea* centers of the human brain and it is directly related with the cosmic currents through the solar plexus of the physical body. The higher *concept* centers of the mind are the switchboard where connections are made, and it is in this way that the psychic body registers its vibrations in the physical, and the physical registers in the psychic--there is a circle of consciousness established by the two minds. This would be of no particular value to us, if it did not prove to us the source of disease, for when we look scientifically and psychologically at disease, we must see that it is simply disassociation between the psychic and the physical selves, and comes as the natural loss of poise, either physically, mentally or psychically.

Watching the play of human disease around us we can soon see that there are two distinct ways by which disassociation of these selves begins; first, through the mind by negative thinking, and second through the emotions by negative feeling.

Our thoughts and our will are the great avenues by which we admit anything into our psychic self, and are also the means by which we exclude all things.

The whole poise of an individual can be destroyed by thoughts of fear, hate, grief and anger; fright has killed and all these states of emotion are simply grades of vibration, setting up inharmonious, psychical activity, and leaving their corresponding effects upon the physical cells.

It is known only too well today by those who seek to know, that back of all such physical conditions as nervousness, prostration, temporary insanity, nervous disorders, pains resembling rheumatism, hay fever, heart troubles, mental symptoms, nervous chills, morbid forebodings and mild mania, there lurks the abnormal activity of the psychic or "thought body" caused by thoughts and feelings acting abnormally upon the vital centers of the nervous system and mind.

New Thought declares that all diseases, except accidental wounds and fractures begin in the psychic or "thought body" as *energy* and then are registered in the physical cells as organic or functional disease.

We might follow this farther in order to satisfy science, but suffice it to go this far, and then seek the value of knowing this: We can see that the only thing that naturally follows is, the healer and patient must be taught how to restore the lost equilibrium of the centers and again poise the life in a creative thought vibration. This is done simply and surely by teaching everyone the *correct* use of the *idea* centers of the human brain and through this he is taught to form such thoughts and produce such ideas as will allow a normal amount of energy to register on both planes, and not permit the psychical mind to drive the human engine on to destruction in a wild waste and explosion of physical, mental or psychical energy.

This is not a long or wearisome task for in the cortex of every brain there are distinct *idea* centers whose business it is to take up ideas built from thoughts, and *will* must follow the idea, and by constantly selecting the thoughts which will produce harmonious vibrations within the psychic and physical selves, we join with the great creative energy of the universe and it flows through us, healing and harmonizing every atom of our body.

The very first step toward healing is to teach the patient to build for himself a *health* consciousness, and this is done by giving him the positive ideas of health instead of the negative ones of disease. We build for him the *idea* of health, hold it firmly in our minds, and project it into his *idea* centers until it registers in his psychic mind; then this is followed by his own increased power of willing, and finally this passes into action and is registered in form.

Ideation, willing and *doing* is the great *health trinity*, and when this is produced, healing must follow. This is the *law* and there is no appeal from it.

When we first meet a diseased person we find his field of consciousness full of all kinds of negative thoughts of disease, worry, fear and anxiety-- these have been persisted in so long that they have weakened both the idea centers and the power of willing. We at once create for him the positive idea motor-form, and if his conscious mind is too weak to receive the impulse, we project it into his psychic mind, helping him hold on to the new idea until his own mind is able to grasp it, and it becomes registered for him.

After he has learned the truth of the abundance of health energy within and without to be aroused into action by the simple law of his own thoughts and feelings, he sets to work to regenerate himself, and he finds that he can really breathe the breath of life into his own nostrils.

After we have seen the scientific side of the real power of healing, then if we want to get health and keep it, we set about studying how to live our life so as to be able to generate thoughts and feelings, at all times, which shall always move us at a creative health vibration. The very next thing for anyone seeking health is to get easy in his everyday life; no one can ever be well and live with every nerve on a tension. We need to know the higher law of life that teaches us that no one put us anywhere but ourselves; that no one is to blame but ourselves for what we have or have not; we get and have in this world just what we have the power to relate with and will get free from the thing we do not like in just the hour that we build something better for ourselves. All we need to do is to cease resisting conditions and agree with our adversary quickly. Freedom, liberty and happiness are not things of the external world; they come from within and we are sad or happy, bound or free, sick or well, not by our external but by our internal conditions.

The sick, nervous, peevish, worrying mind sees everything as positive to itself and must be taught that there is nothing in all the world that has any power over us except that with which we endow it, and it must begin to live under this idea rather than the old foolish one of being controlled by every external condition.

"God hath not given us a spirit of fear but of love and of power and of a sound mind," and with persistent thought culture we can soon form a habit of thought and feeling that will build us away from our old consciousness of disease and pain into a higher law of health and strength.

Good, positive, strong health thoughts are a certain preventive and cure for every kind of disease. Disease and health have absolutely no relation with each other; disease is the expression of a faltering, undeveloped soul life, while health is the expression of a consciousness that has not broken its law of universal recognition.

There are very good people who are sick and very many so-called bad folks who are well; health is not bestowed as a reward of merit, it simply is by the natural universal law, and it exists for those who know how to fulfill the law within their own being. There are many so-called wicked people who live in greater harmony with their wickedness than some so-called Christians can ever do with their religion and goodness. Wholeness or holiness means simply harmony, and harmony inside and outside gives health. Anyone who has health has earned it by obeying the laws that produce it.

Another great factor active in producing inharmonious vibrations and registering destructive energy, is the old thought habit of living under the laws of opposites, thinking thought of health today and of disease tomorrow; to be passing daily between hope and despair. This is sowing mixed thought seeds and cannot help bringing mixed vibrations.

The path to a health consciousness is to get the strong, positive idea of unity and live under the law of similars. To begin at once to affirm union with all the health and strength of the universe and stick to it in the face of all the opposing negative thought vibrations generated within ourselves, or thrown into our minds by others. This can be done by resolutely substituting a health thought for a diseased one; no matter how fast negative thoughts crowd in upon the mind, they can be antidoted by the strong positive affirmation of health.

In order to register *health* vibrations we must *think, feel* and *be* health in mind. The words of health, peace, power and strength do not unfold into radiant flesh and dwell among us through a faltering idea of fear, or vague "perhaps," or "I do hope I shall be well," or "I want to get well," but it demands the eternal I am health now.

Courage, zeal and consecration to the laws of health and freedom from the law of death are not kindled by the halting consciousness full of the law of opposites, but they are the results of *knowing* and *abiding*. When we can in very truth and full of believing say to health, "Thy kingdom come," it *will* come.

Our daily thoughts then become the wires over which there passes into form a finer substance, and our body is rebuilt and fashioned from the indestructible *substance* of the Universe.

The mortal body as we know it in the old thought world, is a thing of earth and lives and suffers earth's calamities, but through the understanding of this New Thought *union* it can be made to become a portion of the *cause* as indestructible as *life* itself, and live and glory in omnipotence.

We are then in the resurrection of the *life*, and the *word* that was *with* God and *was* God, is made *flesh* to dwell among us in glory and full of grace and truth; then we know what Jesus meant when he said, "I tell you of a truth, there be those standing among you who shall not taste of death till they see the Kingdom of God."

The Risen Self

"And entering into the sepulchre they saw a young man sitting on the right side clothed in a long white garment, and he saith unto them, be not affrighted, ye seek Jesus of Nazareth--He is risen! He is not here!"

When we read the Bible with its story of human lives and their great, wonderful mysteries, we find among them, the greatest of all--the marvellous one of the Christ birth and death, and as we read we are amazed at the many confusing ideas of Jesus and His teachings. His disciples themselves did not understand Him, though He sought always to clearly interpret Himself; often when He spoke metaphysically they interpreted Him physically.

There was throughout all the Christ history something so great, so holy, so inclusive that it was too large for them to comprehend, and for all eternal ages, the developing minds of men will be the same. They will keep busy with their attempts at explanation of His life and His words.

Jesus quitted the world in benediction, and He left to those who followed Him and His precepts, a great inextinguishable hope.

It matters little to those who really understand Truth, whether Jesus the Christ lived, or whether He was only a symbol worked out by the imagination of men and priests; be the origin what it may, Christianity *still* stands; and Religion still holds sway after centuries of ridicule and generations of secular and scientific analysis. Something unknown and uninterpreted beats and surges in the hearts of men, and brings into expression in every age the clinging to a great mysterious, wonderful, unseen agency that somehow works its way along the silent avenues of the human soul.

The man Jesus may or may not have lived. Humanity may keep its birthright of contradiction forever on this point, but higher than the limited understanding of the few there lives the Truth of the great Christ spirit which the name Jesus embodied, and which for centuries gone, and centuries to be, will wax strong and flourish in the consciousness of men, as they pass one by one into recognition of it.

Great and sacred was the day of Jesus' birth, and great and sacred was the day of his death, for both revealed the stages of our human selfhood, and both point our minds to deeper meanings of existence.

Jesus' life as we follow it from the manger to the cross was the unmistakable story of the pathway of every human life and each little action was a part of the great mosaic which each life is setting for itself, and from which it shall one day read its own great at-one-ment.

The birth of the Christ consciousness comes to each soul as the dawn of self-awakening. It is the first faint glimmer of a new world, and the first hint the soul of man has of union with its source.

This first dawn of consciousness is purely a possession of the inner self, and those who feel it only follow first by faith. This faith is buffeted and attacked by the things of life until it is tried and becomes steadfast.

In this first dawn of consciousness of the Christ self we are always strangers to ourselves and asleep in the manger of natural things and natural senses. We go on for years, and as consciousness grows stronger we search and search for we know not what; craving pursues us, we go hither and thither seeking, seeking--finding and losing.

The world and the things tangible are never wholly satisfactory in themselves; we know instinctively that they are not all there is, there is a deep, vital something in us that speaks its hidden messages into our being, and we are driven on from sensation to sensation, crying for that open sesame of union which will bring peace to our soul.

Then passing into deeper unfoldment we come into the real work of life, we meet with responsibilities and its experiences; we are baffled again, buffeted, besieged by the perplexities of doubt and fear and human discontent and we feel that, strive as we will, we are not yet at home.

The ten thousand things of the human life entangle us,--the touch of sickness, the expressions of so-called sin,--the baffling consequences of our seeming mistakes,--all these draw us from the cradle of unconsciousness out into the vital power of a self-conscious life, and push us onward to our union with Cosmic Consciousness, or the risen Christ.

On the self-conscious plane life goes on, driven on every side by human experiences and at last turns back upon itself, and then in the Gethsemane of its own making, it stands where earth and its perplexing joys are lost and heaven and its hidden joys are yet unknown, and then facing the expressions of its now half-revealed consciousness it cries out from the depth of its soul's despair, "If it is possible, let this cup pass," and it does not see the purpose in Gethsemane.

Human life at this stage of unfoldment has *fixed laws*, and the soul meets in them the inexorable command to pass on to its own crucifixion, the worked out sentence of its own judgments, and it goes onward bearing its own cross which is built from the consequences of the laws with which it has related.

The laws of human self-consciousness are hard to work out; each life faces sometime, somewhere the proof of itself. There comes a day to all when anything that is less than the truth slips off, and the soul stands bare at the bar of the universal justice ready to be judged by the laws which it has made for itself.

There are hours of human crucifixion that it were well to die on, for the soul that wanders back from these fierce Mounts of Transfiguration has paid the price of human transgression of law by human pain, and is purged and cleaned by the fierce fire of its own igniting.

The path of human living out leads every life up the steps of Calvary carrying its own Cross and it plaits the thorns and pierces the side of "Him who in our life again is spit upon and crucified" until, at last, the great human God-self within us is released through transmutation, and the grave clothes of our dead self no longer entomb us; then the resurrection day is at hand, and the Consciousness of God bursts into the self-conscious mind, and the stone is rolled away from the sepulchre.

The human mind bursts forth in illumination and it passes with the Christ birth on to the table-land of human comprehension and revelation of its infinite union.

In this moment of glorified illumination we feel and know that every moment behind us has been that this hour may be; we feel then that every moment is a special moment; every life a special life, protected by the all life, and that everything on our human pathway, high or low, has led us on to this supreme moment of conscious union with our God.

When the Christ Consciousness is risen within us, we feel the universality of life written everywhere on everything; there is but one starting point for all thought--God. There is but one ending place for all human faith--God.

We are filled with a keener sense of the oneness of life, and we are thrilled again and again by the nearness and greatness of God in the world which He projected from Himself.

The Father which we sought in self-consciousness has become real and tangible, and the sense of everlasting unity is in our hearts.

With this great God-self alive within us, we never fear that God will ever pass away from any part of his Creation. We know too well, then, the truth that "as it was in the beginning, is now, and ever shall be, world without end," earth is destined to become a heaven in the lives of men as fast as they develop to the place of understanding, and find the real holy ground within the center of their own being.

God, or the Universal Cosmic Consciousness, has always been revealed to men through the risen Christ consciousness within the self. The men of old who walked with Him were those who had lifted their personal mind to the level of the Universal Mind, so that from the shores of the Infinite Wisdom great thought waves of Love, Truth and Peace beat in on them and filled them, and their lives became a center of illumination for all.

There never was and there never can be any conflict between the power of human consciousness and God consciousness. Truth is always Truth, and Truth in the hearts of men build them back into the Great Harmony.

The Absolute never contradicts itself; as fast as lives are unfolded to the Christ Consciousness, they leave the old thought life like an empty tomb and push themselves into a glorious human expression, just as the Easter lily rising above the dust and mould of earth, pushes itself upward into the clear sunlight of a world where flowers are revealed, just so the soul pushes on through consciousness and self-consciousness, into the glory of the risen Godhood.

We can hear the voice of the Universal calling us through our Christ Consciousness today, just as it called to men throughout the ages, and we know that everything that throbs with natural life or comes into objective expression in our human world, is really only the voice of the Universal Cosmic mind speaking in the holy language of the human heart.

Every experience, every heartache, every joy, every despair, every pulse-beat is only the text by which the great child mind of the world is spelling out *God*.

The Risen Self comes into realization of the great white light of the soul, and it enables us to see *all* life in its completeness. Human effort and human endeavor glow with an unexpected radiance when seen from the table-land of the risen truth.

The human soul then rejoices in its Divine possibilities. Jesus said: "I do always the things that pleaseth the Father," and the voice from heaven said: "This is my beloved son in whom I am well pleased."

When we turn to those who ask for proof of the risen Christ-self within us, we have only to point to them the empty tomb of the old lives which men everywhere leave behind them. If we desire we can go farther and point them to the production of those in whom this great consciousness is waking; all human life that is alive with thought and faith and deed, is vibrant with a great vital spiritual force.

The signs of God Consciousness and the conscious union of God and men is rampant everywhere in the natural world. Every factory, every steamship, every invention, every composition, everything in form sets its seal upon the genuineness of the existence of the spiritual exaltation of the minds of men, and higher than the things of the natural world, there stands the achievements of the mental and inspirational souls; the libraries with their tens of thousands of written pages, the art museums and galleries of precious dreams; all over the world there are hung on walls and chiselled into glistening marble the story of the glory-gazing of some Christ-illumined soul. And again sounded forth from thousands of churches each Sabbath morning, there is swelling out majestic songs sung by myriads of voices now, but sung *first* in the silence of some dim, deep soul-dream, in the Christ consciousness of some risen mind. That grand harmony was born on the table-lands of human illumination, registered on the human brain, and worked out into tangible form here on earth to bear witness to the home-land of the God-man.

Christ consciousness is the final destiny of every soul; it is what we really live by and today we know, as never before, that in order to advance and grow, we must consecrate and bring it here and now, into its fullest expression in our life.

There are bound to be born, at first, many things on this table-land of new understanding that will be worked out indifferently by our limited brain, and when challenged by the strain and stress of life they will depart because they will be unable in their present form to answer to the great world's need. But increasing consciousness makes everything more powerful, and as we go on we learn to build sublime and lasting things, to stand the test of time because they have their root, not in the old thought self, but in the unfolded risen self, and they are grappled to the heart of the very Rock of Ages.

Standing, then, risen from the dust world of our old defeats, our human minds receive new illuminations and rejoice in them. Law becomes the essence of our daily living and the mind of man the direct inspiration of the Almighty. We dare to trust our risen mind to the uttermost for in it is God himself enshrined.

In this new spiritual perception we rely more and more on our intuitions, illumination and revelation, for it is human Godness, backed by the strength of unnumbered hosts of higher consciousness.

We know at last that all our daily living is not a matter of outward signs but of inward sight; all external things may contradict us, yet in sublime confidence we shape our way while the Christ voice within us speaks forth its messages, telling us all the holy and uplifting stories of our daily life. Over the trials and wreckage of our common years we follow it; out from a silence that is known only to ourselves we bring the lessons that have burnt their truth into our souls.

In the power of this risen self we stand with our faces upturned, with our whole life opened to God, and human effort, human growth, human hope, love, joy,--all are joined in the sense of Divine resurrection.

This is the consciousness of God in the human soul; this is the Resurrection morning and it makes us now the Sons of God, and from the darkness of our Old Thought growth we lift our hearts away into a new Life Divine. We open our eyes in the radiance of a light that never grows dim, then standing with an all-seeing soul vision, we can point to the long years behind us through which we have worked out our soul's salvation and closing the door on the empty tomb of our dead self we say with all the serenity of our new-found God-consciousness:

"I know whom you seek. He is not here. He is Risen!"

Transcendentalism

Transcendentalism is today the one subject which is demanding the greatest attention. The race mind is beginning to think in words of transcendental language rather than in the old law of science and philosophy, and all the light of modern investigation centres round the one who declares himself a transcendentalist.

We may say that a man is a scientist, a philosopher or a materialist, and the world will know at once what we mean, but if we say that he is a transcendentalist we leave an open doorway for investigation; there is something yet to be learned about him, something that no one knows about but himself.

Anyone can easily define a scientist, a philosopher and a psychologist, but they halt in more or less indecision when they are asked to define a transcendentalist, and it is only when we understand that a transcendentalist is one who has extended his normal consciousness into relationship with the deeper laws of the universe, so that he uses naturally these laws and is perfectly familiar and at home in states of consciousness which the rest of the world call supernatural, and with which they are entirely unfamiliar, that we can come to a true definition of the transcendentalist.

Transcendentalism has been a part of race unfolding since time began, and will continue to be throughout all race evolution.

In the old civilization we studied the transcendentalist and transcendentalism from an entirely different view-point than we do today.

Transcendentalism is a state of consciousness and man evolves into it out of the natural states of his own mind. No one is to blame that he is, or is not, a transcendentalist. He becomes one not alone because he wills to become, but also because he is one with the divine law of creation and the God-consciousness within him pushes him on through one state of unfoldment to another.

There are two expressions of universal and finite mind, one is the objective, the revealed, the apparent, and one is the subjective, the concealed, the absolute.

The objective side of mind belongs to the surface consciousness of man, and is in itself a distinct state of existence, it is bounded on every side by its own laws, and commands its own obedience. The subjective side of life belongs to the inner side of mind and is also a distinct state of existence bounded by itself and the laws of its own kingdom, and without a deep knowledge of universal law, man has little power of connecting these two strong zones of consciousness.

Studying life in the light of our modern understanding, we find that man passes by natural law through the objective, the surface zone, then on to the subjective or inner zone, and then to a centralized position between both zones where he lives, moves and has being in both zones, uniting the laws of the two kingdoms into a new zone of consciousness, then using the laws of both, he passes at will to the very edge of matter, and back to the very center of the cosmic mind; standing here in life's master position, he is lord of both zones. This middle zone of power and mastery is the path of the modern transcendentalist, and the one who walks it and lives in unification with its laws is the *modern transcendentalist* of the new civilization. It has been written--

"For wide is the gate, and broad is the way that leadeth to destruction, and many there be who go in thereat" because

"Straight is the gate, and narrow is the way which leadeth unto Life."

We know today that this is true, for on the broad path of the objective life man must pass through the law of change which destroys, that it may create again and through which he is crowded on to seek the narrow path of subjective senses which are built on the law of verities.

Man's first lessons are in the objective zone of mind, and he remains positive in this zone until he masters its laws and the lessons which they bring.

In this objective zone of mind we find the mass man of the old civilization, he is in the *broad way* of the surface consciousness, and in his midst there dwells the specialized individuals who are approaching the central zones of mind; they are called the scientist, the physicist, the materialist, the agnostic, the mentalist, the reasoner, and the atheist, all true and perfect for their type but all more or less unconscious of the latent states of mind within themselves and the universe to which they must some day respond.

As human consciousness intensifies through use, man finds himself passing on through his surface zones to the concealed states of mind within himself, "the narrow way," and slowly, almost unconsciously at first, he begins manifesting the law of these zones. In these states of mind we find the philosopher, the idealist, the emotionalist, the psychist, the sensitive, the intuitionist, the revelator, the transcendentalist and the seer.

Watching race evolution we see that the day of surface consciousness and its power is waning only as it is controlled and manipulated through the subjective states of man's mind. The hour for subjective research and subjective introspection is at hand,--men have mastered the external world and its laws, and are now following the cosmic urge which is pushing them toward the center and away from the *apparent* to the *absolute* laws of life.

The external evolution of form is complete for this hour; men go down into the bowels of the earth, they sail the seas, they mount the air on wings, and the external world has seen "the son of man coming in clouds of glory" and now the eternal man must have his hour, and come in "trailing robes of power and brightness," to pour new revelation through the external world and its laws.

Books, paintings, pictures, science, music have all had their day in external exaltation, and now the attention of man is mounting higher and turning inward; the study of the surface and sub-consciousness has been transferred, and while part of the world's eyes are yet peering through the microscope at the *sub-life* and plenty are looking at the laws of life around them, the transcendentalist with these truths locked fast in his mind, is turning to the undiscovered states within himself, and is everywhere launching out into the unfathomed states of the supra-mind of man.

Man has evolved like a planet through the stone age of mind and today with the planet in the vibratory zone of water and *air* he has risen with it into the transcendent states of his own being.

Many transcendentalists are living so naturally in the beginning manifestations of the supra-mind that they hardly recognize them as uncommon and the world is becoming peopled with a race of supra-men and supra-women who are using the subtle laws of the transcendentalists of the past, but not using them *alone,* or in *hidden cloisters,* or through separate states of living, but using them as simple human attributes of their own mind, and using them in the common marts of the surface life with more real understanding than did the olden transcendentalist in his specialized separated environment, assisted by *secluded study* and *special opportunities.*

The modern transcendentalist is a post graduate of the surface consciousness, and uses it as simply a wireless machine with which he registers his deeper perceptions, and with it links himself and his revelation naturally to the natural world. He stands in natural communion with both zones, and in this communion with deeper laws he attains a supra-power, he walks his human pathway in human form, but he manipulates his surface life with the power born of his supra-wisdom.

The modern transcendentalists form the corner-stones of the new civilization. "For the new age will come quickly to its birth when this His world, will know itself divine" and in this new civilization the mass man will have for his surface consciousness, the deep subtle union of both zones, and the specialized teacher, leader and messenger of this new age, will forge ahead on the great white way of prophecy and seership which is born from the union of the finite and infinite mind.

To the mind of the old civilization this will not seem true, for it is still in the swaddling clothes of its old inheritance; in the thoughts of the past, man and God, matter and spirit, finite and infinite have been so long divorced and separated that it will be found difficult to accept the union of incense and worship and reverence in the same breath with the real, the apparent and the formed, but this is the hour for higher prophecy, and that hour when the "lion and the lamb shall lie down together."

To those who are really able to read the signs of the times, human consciousness everywhere offers the greatest proof of this truth, for looking with eyes that can see, we find that every individual is in possession of eight distinct states of consciousness with which he can operate in the subjective and objective zones.

There may be still greater stretches of the human mind into union with the universal which the oncoming races will discover, but that there are eight distinct levels of mind activity many know because they have touched them and know them within themselves.

Some minds are active in one, some in two, some in three, and some in four, and some are more or less distinct in all.

The mass man of the new civilization is awake in the *third* and *fourth* dimensions of his mind, and those in higher reaches are awake in the *fifth* and *sixth*, a few are in the *seventh* and *eighth*, but the rank and file are familiar to some degree with all these states.

The first or surface mind of man is in itself only cell consciousness, touched by man's own intellect, and it is known as *instinct*, his second expression of mind is known as *reason*, the third is *emotion* or *feeling*, and the fourth is instinct, reason and emotion blended into one, and called *intuition*. The fifth and sixth are above the plane of thought and feeling and includes them in a still higher intensification; here thinking ceases and *registration* is the law, and here is where *revelation* is born. The seventh and eighth are still supra reaches of man's mind, and include the union or surface consciousness with the higher states, in which the brain becomes the wireless machine, through which flashes of divine wisdom comes; this is called *Prophecy* and *Seership* and this is the product of the "mirror-mind."

There are bodies and atmospheres to fit each transcendent state of mind, and the transcendentalist can suspend any, or all of his states of mind, one after another, and pass into direct atonement with any level with which he wishes to function; he can at will live in a new world, and speak with a new tongue, and fill his surface mind with a glory not its own, "but which it had with Him before the world was."

These new states of mind in action extends man's world into the wider reaches of the universal and adds to him new levels of wisdom and power.

There are reaches of intelligence far below and beyond the common intelligence as the microscope and the telescope have shown, and at the fourth and fifth dimension of consciousness man dispenses with all material aids and uses the adjustments of his own being. He has found the eyes, the ears, and the understanding of the supra-self, and by suspending his surface mind through concentration and meditation he can enter any sphere of thought at will and be in the land of clairvoyance, clairaudience, and in the astral and atmospherian, or pass farther out and register in his surface brain the wonders and laws of etherian, and celestial worlds. He is at one with the world of the sensitive, the impressionist and the medium, and in the deeper states of vision he can see and read the memory tablets of the universe. In the higher registrations he becomes cosmo-voyant and cosmo-audient, he can see and hear through space and through ethers as the common eye looks through air. These are not special gifts from God, but simply the gifts man gives himself through the conscious use of what is already in his possession.

The power to extend sight and hearing far above and below the so-called senses is latent within every individual and when the point of transcendental development is reached he uses it naturally.

There are some people who can see birds in the air, ships at sea, stars in the sky, while others standing beside them see only empty space. Just so there are many everywhere on life's pathway who can extend their normal vision and hearing to such an intensified vibratory rate that it not only includes all the things of the physical plane but the things of the finer ethers.

The transcendentalist standing on the streets of New York can extend his vision and look at a street or building in Chicago or Cairo or London, while the surface man alongside of him can scarcely read the signs on the other side of the street.

The modern transcendentalist does only what the surface man does--he looks to see and brings one hundred percent of his vision to bear upon his desire, while the surface man has less than ten percent of himself in action and that *only* on one plane.

There are enough people on the planet today who can use these deep states of mind, and induce the extended vision and hearing at will to make it more than a mere hypothetical conclusion; there are X-ray beings among us who have come into contact with a great fundamental principle both within and without themselves.

The time will come in the near future, when the operator with the Roentgen ray will stand beside his machine and look with wide open eyes and find the X-ray in his own vision, and will work unlimited by the bondage of his material machine.

Comparing the modern transcendentalist and his pathway with that of the olden transcendentalist with his ascent of travail and pain, we find a profound satisfaction in the picture of power, peace and love of the modern supra-man.

The pathway of the elder supra-man was one of crucifixion, self-denial, renunciation, affliction, poverty, disease and self-mortification. He found the steps to the higher consciousness and its power only through slow self-conquest and comradeship with pain, and this was the inheritance he handed down through the centuries. To think in terms of mystical wisdom meant human denial of all sentient life. Unification was bought through total consecration to the subjective and the absolute, in which the diverse could have no part.

Today "we are free where our sires were serfs, we can see where He left them blind," and we know that God-consciousness is man's immortal birthright and that the son of man must somewhere on his pathway become the son of God, and as he passes on in his unfoldment he will contact every atom of God-mind in all lines of expression, and from the world of matter he will turn in time naturally to those levels of mind which lead him into reverence, illumination and worship, and through this he finds the whole of life.

Man in his immersion into cosmic consciousness puts forth profound tests of his oneness and faces life in larger and larger proportions, and as he ascends he carries all with him, so that he can give back to all a profound and heroic response.

Every man is transcendent when the hour dawns for his transcendent self to tremble into action.

With these wider reaches of consciousness the modern transcendentalist finds the larger life and the true way of living, and in this brings the new message of the "One life in all and through all" into the mass mind, and the new song of joy and thanksgiving into their hearts. He is never sad, never agonizing, never renouncing; he has made contact with all life and through this with the universal joy; there is no denial, no separateness,--there is "no more crying," he conquers and ascends not through separateness but through increasing degrees of union. He lives in glad comradeship with God, in joy and perfected self-expression, both in the objective and in the subjective world.

The ancient transcendentalist was always sad, always separate, always worshipping in beatific loneliness, in seclusion and renunciation of the world; the modern supra-man passes from end to end of the pole of being and stops at any point and functions normally. "He stands and works, then kneels and prays." He is lord of the outside external world and partaker of all its divine joys and pleasures, and he is lord of all the deeper reaches of subjective consciousness within himself and the absolute in which he lives, and he brings out from these deeper levels all the intensified power of illumination and revelation, and pours it over his daily pathway illumining it with a glory not its own.

Many olden transcendentalists lived on in entranced states of divine wisdom with diseased flesh and bodies that shrieked with pain, while they mortified and rejected that divine wisdom. The modern transcendentalist brings all his God-consciousness to bear upon his flesh and raises it to the transcendent heights of his own mind and heals it until bone and muscle and tissues gleam and scintillate with a new found beauty and youth.

The olden transcendentalist dragged on in barren cells and dreary poverty in order not to divert his glorified vision of the formless by the beauty of the *ever present form*; the modern transcendentalist brings his higher laws into play, conquers his poverty and commands around himself the beauty and luxury and freedom of the world of form, and it speaks to him in matchless raiment, luxuriant flowers, gems, material comforts and soft ease. He lives in rapturous companionship with the glory and beauty and majesty of God in the world *He has projected from Himself*, and with this beneath him, he can rise to the very pinnacle of infinite selfhood.

The olden transcendentalist, ascending into the transcendental heights of his own mind, ascended alone, and from these obscure heights he shed his wisdom back upon the evolving race; he was pioneer in the lands of cosmic consciousness and the first revelator of the path; he showed the race that the path was there to tread, and his messages have fallen as a benediction on the race mind even while he himself bought his wisdom with pain, renunciation and suffering built from the limited recognition of his own mind.

The path winds onward and upward still, but the feet of those climbing it today are led by still waters and in the paths of righteousness. They are no longer in the part but are in the middle of the Divine Channel of God-consciousness. To know *one* part was the mission of the *past*; to know *all parts* and join them in a divine unity is the mission of the *present*.

The modern transcendentalist does not love life less, he loves it more! The world is alive with a new majesty; the passing multitude, the passing face, every human attribute of life calls forth from him a deeper interpretation; he walks out into the race mind, and with the power of a new word, and a new touch heals it from its infirmity. He does in truth give "absent treatments," and his word is accomplished; the old diseased flesh transmutes in answer to his command. He speaks to the barren walls of poverty and they stretch away into stately halls, for he knows that wherever man posits his consciousness, substance must gather round it; his new words of power and majesty fall like a benediction on the heart of the listening multitudes, and they turn round to face a new tomorrow with a new hope born of a larger understanding.

The transcendentalist walks often in our midst; sometimes he assumes the simplicity of a child to disguise the larger stretches of power within him, but he is out upon the pathway strong and beautiful, wholly replete with promises of perfection, doing the work of the human.

There is a royal road from *appearance* to *reality*, from *objective* to *subjective*, from the limited to the absolute.

Difference is merging into one *great white way* through which the new civilization is thronging, led by the intensified vision of the supra-minds.

Unity has carried man above all things of human law, and he has found that Mighty Force of which all is a part, and he is out into the land of "naked visions" and *knows*.

He dwells securely upon the height and has ceased the long fight with the objective half of himself; he is one with matter because he has transcended and absorbed it; he is centralized in the formless and spiritualized in the formed, and can say from the level of his own Christ consciousness:

"I and my Father are one."

"All that my Father hath is mine."

The Psychology Of Insanity

With the ever present increase of insanity, it is not only interesting but important that the subject of insanity should be studied from all viewpoints, and anything which can be contributed that will help in controlling or curing it, should be accepted as good material.

It is an apparent fact that the multitude knows very little about the cause of insanity and less about the cure. Investigation has in the past been directed to the physical side of the disease, and many of the insane hospitals are examples of physical comfort and perfect physical attention, but they are also living examples of the fact that to house, feed and clothe the demented does not necessarily mean a cure, and a call for deeper understanding is imperative.

Civilization needs each individual as a unit in the great working force of life, and those who need to be taken care of by a State take away a legitimate support and add just that much more to the burden of the State.

A civilization which can increase the independence of the individual and lessen the responsibility of the State is one to be directly desired.

Insanity calls for a closer study than has ever been given and only through a deeper realization of its cause, can a cure be brought about and individuals rendered of value to themselves and the country.

Insanity is nothing more or less than disassociated states of mind and need not in reality be any more serious than errors of refraction of vision, faulty locomotion or lack of coordination. It comes because individuals know nothing of the psychology of themselves or their own minds and is the result of over-intensified mental and physical activity and loss of poise, physically, mentally and psychically. The insane are not capable of understanding themselves, and up to the present day there are very few who are able to understand them.

The nurses, matrons and physicians of a great asylum are powerless to assist them because of their own ignorance of the true laws of psychology. The cases which simple, natural, physical methods will assist, are cured, but thousands of others are allowed to drag along with the dreadful stigmata of "hopelessly insane."

Insanity is increasing because civilization is changing, and conditions are changing. As conditions change the minds of men change and today subjective states of mind in the individual are becoming intensified. Instinct, reason, emotion, intuition, revelation and prophecy are all struggling for expression; unrelated and misunderstood they become disease; related and understood they can be made to bring forth a new race with new extensive reaches of intelligence.

There are few people so stupid but that they can testify to the conflicting states of emotions within themselves and there are many people who are perfectly familiar with states of consciousness with which many other people are entirely unfamiliar.

Wherever we go we are continually confronted with what the world calls "freaky" or "eccentric" people, and these people are found in all degrees from the slightly odd folks to those filling the asylums, and strange as it may seem, no matter how queer they may appear to other people, they never seem so to themselves.

There are many families with members whom the rest call irrational, irresponsible or "black sheep." Again, there are many families who have one child who, from the time of its birth, has called for methods of management entirely different from those used for the other children. There are many little sensitive creatures who are afraid of the dark and who have queer ideas and odd ways, and there are delicate little people who have bodies so finely organized that they are nearly broke into pieces with the natural things which the other members never notice. They are born sensitives and remain sensitives to the end of their lives, and only as they can be taught the truth about themselves can they be rescued from some form of mental disturbances.

These people as they grow older, become what is termed "psychics"; they are over-intensified in some of their deeper states of mind. They are not alone the product of civilization, but the product of race evolution. Many of them pass on in semi-normal states of self-support, but they are a well known class, and they are more or less unsuccessful in supporting themselves along natural lines of labor, and if they inherit wealth they run into vagaries and often degenerate lines of living; they squander their all and die in charity.

The common business world is full of psychics and it is correspondingly full of failures for this is not a faculty that makes for success or power with material things.

Psychics who are only slightly disassociated are always a source of annoyance to their friends, and often looked upon as irresponsible, and have to be looked after by some one who has patience enough to be with them, and often they are passed along as having an artistic temperament.

As long as their peculiar development does not interfere with normal action they are unmolested by the public. It is only when deeper states of mind become so over-intensified that they lose their normal relationship to normal things of the world that they are put under control. They are called paranoics, melancholics, demented and insane. A correct mental training would teach them to re-associate their mind and to live a moderately normal life, at least. All drunkards and drug fiends are psychics; degenerates are also psychics. These conditions are simply the result of loss of polarity of normal mind centers, resulting in the conflict of states of consciousness within themselves.

There are also many psychics in the ignorant and undeveloped classes. The witch women and seers, and many of the colored races are psychic. In the past, these people were looked upon as witches and their words and works were known as "witchcraft."

There are many psychics who are also great geniuses. Lord Byron and the "Mad Painter" of Belgium were psychics. History is rife and galleries of art and temples of literature stand as testimonials to some of the constructive productions of their minds, but beside them run dark stories born of their psychic uncertainty.

Criminals of certain types are psychics with no power of physical control and they pass into subjective control and live and do the things that are given them to do from the psychical mind and are often ignorant of their own condition.

Those whom the medical profession call paranoics are simply psychics, over-developed in the subjective faculties--a prey to all the disembodied forces of the subjective plane, and also to every floating thought on the physical plane; they are obsessed by ideas from within and without and their actions bear witness to this statement. Some very meddlesome women, and those who are the terror of a quiet community, are nearly always those who are in the control of the slower psychic forces and unable to consciously direct their own normal states of mind.

In science the psychics are called diseased. Science gives all actions a physical basis, but it is time to know that abnormal states of consciousness, that are only changes in the functional side of the mind and which have no apparent physical basis, are found in thousands.

Neurasthenics and psychasthenics present the mildest picture of disordered states of mind. All neurasthenics and psychasthenics are psychics and their diseases can only be fully understood by the psychologist. The scientist has long ago exhausted his knowledge of the cause and cure of these diseases and this is why all branches of metaphysical healing are overcrowded.

To understand this abnormal thing called "insanity," one must fully understand the normal, called "sanity." There are four distinct states of consciousness in every individual; these must be kept co-related and all of them manifest through the common everyday mind. These four states of consciousness are *instinct, reason, emotion* and *intuition*. These four states of consciousness are *functions* of the normal mind. When a patient becomes over-intensified in either one of these parts of the mind, mental disease results. The psychic is over-intensified in the emotional and intuitional functions of his mind, thus rendering his common sense states *uncommon*, and according to the degree of over-activity, he is either a "freak," a creature of "temperament," a "genius" or a "dementia."

The ordinarily insane individual has lost all relationship with his natural, instinctive and reasoning mind. He is disassociated. Reason, instinct, emotion and intuition are all in conflict within him. The emotional and intuitional faculties overfunctioning distort his common understanding. His idea centers are not able to distinguish between the real and the unreal in thoughts. He becomes possessed and obsessed by ideas born of emotion and intuition that have no foundation in fact, and as time goes on, he loses complete control of his idea centers.

Every individual has definite idea centers within his own brain, and it is through these centers that ideas are coordinated, received or rejected. As over-intensification of feeling and emotion goes on, the normal action of the idea centers is interfered with and the individual has superinduced emotional and intuitional states which are no longer guarded by reason and thought. The emotion senses a purely imaginary condition and the idea centers have no power to reduce it to truth. As time goes on, all power of association is lost and the individual passes along, the plaything of his subjective states of mind. As he becomes more and more intensified subjectively, he opens the deep psychic currents both within and without himself, and loses his connection with his common mind and his physical body, and becomes a prey to all the psychic currents.

There are lives everywhere open to subjective thought currents, and all unknown to themselves they are allowing themselves to become disintegrated by the daily and hourly response they are giving to the stimulus of a plane they should master instead of allowing it to master them.

The psychic plane may become a pathway to power, or it may become the open doorway to a body and mind full of disease, insanity and absolute loss of power and poise.

There are many patients confined in the asylums today, who would never have been there, and who would be released and cured, if those in charge fully understood the truth of this unnaturally natural development and directed their attention to its control.

The first truth is, people are born into what is to them natural relationship with this psychic plane and go on for years misunderstood, pained and repressed, unable to rescue themselves from what they do not understand, and in the end the physical body does become diseased by the continual inroads of strain and repression; functional disorder and anatomical changes result. The farmer's wife loses her mental balance through repression of the fine emotional, intuitional side of her mind which finds no expression in the dull environment of the farm. The over-worked mother loses her mental poise; disassociation follows over-stimulation of the practical and repression of the artistic; and in emotional patients exaggerated states of feeling go on into greater disassociation for lack of strong sensible thought control.

And the second truth is, that many are born so close in relationship to the unseen plane and in such psychical correspondence, that some slight thing which weakens the will-power--sorrow, a disease that devitalizes the physical, some shock, or some prolonged or strained mental condition, breaks down the remaining law of separation, and the life is astray in the psychical world, manifesting abnormal, physical laws.

There is one great connecting link between the physical and the psychical through which all abnormal conditions can be corrected, and this is will power. When this power of will is broken, the life must become a manifestation of error, according to the generally accepted idea of normal relationship.

The will-power of an individual is dependent upon his ideation. Weaken his power to carry an idea, and his will grows correspondingly weak; the *will* must *follow* the idea; it is not a separate entity--*will* only exists in *partnership* with the *idea*.

Ideation, willing and *motion* are the great human trinity from which everything else originates. When we inspect our minds, we find that a voluntary motion is always preceded by the idea of that motion. The idea is first and the will follows the idea. Ideas have definite sensory centers in the cortex of the brain and conscious ideation may be induced to produce a particular form of willing. All voluntary action depends, first, upon the ideas of action, then the willing to do, then the doing. The will-power, in its accelerating and restraining impulses, is modified by the degree of the intensity of the idea. Grief, fear, worry, anger, despondency, anxiety, hate, resistance are all negative ideas that weaken the idea centers and produce weakness of willing. These ideas persisted in at first produce indecision and after a while absolute inaction because the patient has lost the perfect co-relation of his idea centers, which associate instinct, reason, emotion and intuition.

In order to get complete control of the will we must get complete control of the idea centers and induce strong, positive ideas which the will cannot refuse to follow.

When we associate all states of consciousness--instinct, reason, emotion, and intuition, in one strong, centralized idea, it is impossible for physical expression to do anything else than follow this idea.

When one has come into certain conditions of negativeness in any part of his mind, and continues in it for any length of time, it takes more than his own power to modify these intensified conditions and bring about an inhibiting power of mind which will crowd them out, and allow the idea centers to receive a new thought-form and intensify it so that the will can pass it into action.

The abnormal individual is always weak in obeying his ideas and carrying out his impulse because there is a dissociation of idea centers and his mind becomes mixed in its responses and he cannot make for a true, harmonious expression on all of the planes of mind within himself--this is the condition of the neurasthenic and psychasthenic, and he needs some mind stronger than his own to hold his ideas true to what he knows to be true.

The first lesson for the diseased mental patient to learn is that if he wants to keep his mental balance or restore it, he must first inhibit all negative ideation and refuse to allow himself to be driven into wild bursts of psychical or mental energy along any one line. He must force himself to interest his mind in other things and to inhibit the over-active states of thinking. This is best done by a complete change of environment, and often a change of friends. Friends and environment, more than any other things, have the greatest power of keeping the mind intensified in its old thought ruts.

There is little hope of receiving a new ideation and acting upon it, when one allows himself day after day to drag through the same central sensations and receive the same nerve impulses, and register the same responses. By removing to a new environment, and substituting new mental and psychical vibrations the old states of consciousness are allowed to rest while a new unworked state of mind begins.

Psychical development is not a disease; it is an attribute of individual growth; no one is to blame if he has it or has it not; all that anyone needs to know is the truth about it and just how to control it and direct it. Subjective hearing and vision come just as naturally to us as life and death--they are a part of the great plan of unfoldment.

In teaching man to co-relate his many states of developing consciousness into one powerful state of mind, we use our everyday common sense. We give him a place of mental power and after such training he opens or shuts his mind to suit himself; he can live in either extension of consciousness at will and extending his understanding into the transcendent side of his own mind, he can become the modern mystic or seer. He can function in the purely material side of himself or he can become an intensified psychic or mystic by simply suspending and intensifying different centers within himself.

Concentration, centralization in ideas, conscious mental substitution, creation of strong mental ideas, and psychic displacement of the negative with the positive, both by the patient within himself and from the attendant or physician without, will bring insanity under control.

When men fully understand their own mind's scope, they will find that what the world calls un-natural states of consciousness, are only cerebral and psychic disassociation.

The greater freedom of the race, and the cure and control of insanity will be found in the deeper study of *all* levels of mind rather than the one or the few. Only as physical science unites with metaphysical, and these both unite with scientific psychical investigation, will humanity pass toward a solution of its insanity problems. Insanity, delusions, hallucinations, the so-called mental diseases will pass just because they have been naturally displaced by our higher scientific preventive psycho-therapy.

The asylum doors will only open as a place of refuge where men and women will be taught the psychology of the self; there will be *schools* not *cells*. Outside the asylum doors there will be an ever increasing crowd of intelligent men and women psychologists, who will be awake to the first hint of psychic disassociation in an individual. With keen insight and scientific direction, they will teach the beginning paranoic, melancholic, neurasthenic, clairvoyant and psychasthenic the truth about themselves and the first hint of disassociation will be replaced by association, and rest homes, asylums and sanitarium doors will close forever!

The Law Eternal

"For since the fathers fell asleep all things continue as they were from the Creation."

Whenever we read the stories in the Bible, our minds are held with a deep interest, for through all its pages and in all its words, there breathes out the history of the hopes, dreams and aspirations of human hearts, and above every other story or hope or dream, there stands first in absorbing interest the history of the man Jesus, with his wonderfully inspired life. This wonderful Christ life as given in history is a benediction to the world, and his teachings have given us a great inextinguishable hope. In all his history there is one profound principle that never becomes obscured, and that is his eternal adherence to the Law of Life. He never forgot to speak the word that should show the true laws of Cause and Effect.

Nearly all the people of his day followed the letter of his word and not the spirit. When he spoke in parables they interpreted in fact, and even when he said: "I go to prepare a place for you, and if I go and prepare a place, I will come again and receive ye unto myself, that where I am, there ye may be also," they believed and interpreted it to mean really material facts, and began to build up their finite hope for a future kingdom, totally blind to the deep subjective law of his spoken word.

They really believed that if they waited a few years, at most, Jesus would return unto them, and in triumph and power gather them together and raise up a community of peace and love in this earth plane. They believed that through this they would become monarchs of a new world. Nothing in their minds revealed the impossibility of material form without fundamental facts beneath them.

The sick and suffering and discouraged of every class, knowing nothing of the higher laws, laid this hope to their hearts, and filled with a courage built on this belief, they taught themselves to stand silent beneath scorn and persecution, feeling inwardly, that when the hour of Christ's return came, their life would suddenly become powerful through some new dispensation.

The years came and went, one after another the apostles died with their hope still in their hearts; at last, only the lengthened life of John was left on which to hang expectancy, then he, too, died and the Jesus of their hope had not returned. Even then the church was reluctant to give up its teaching of the letter and it still held, that even while a few followers remained whose term reached back to Christ's time, it was not too late for his return, and the son of man might yet be sustained in his earthly kingdom.

Time went on until even the oldest memories of the promises passed; change after change came, and man could no longer find a finite place for his faith and trust, and then, as human life was pushed on by the great resistless ebb-tide of the Infinite, those who were still clinging to this false hope, broke forth in a wail of despair, and they cried, "Where is the promise of His coming?" "For since the fathers fell asleep, all things continue as they were from the creation."

We who read their history today and know the truth of Life's finer relationships, cannot but feel a pity for their failure, and the lingering death of their expectancy, even while we see that it was built on superficial human understanding.

In the great unrelated, ignorant hope of these people, we can read in letters of fire, the proof of the certainty of disappointment of every human hope that has not its conscious union with the great universal Laws of Life.

We can see now with the calm vision of those who have no part in their superstition that their hope was never built on the understanding and wisdom of creation, but upon weak, human desires and narrow personal expectation.

It can easily be seen that under the great Law Eternal it was not possible, that after training only a small part of the human race-thought there could be a return, a king of any sort, or that there could follow the perfecting of the race in any such a narrow, limited, personal way.

When Truth has become revealed to the minds of men, they at once see that laws remain, and that the human race is bound to fit itself to these, and looking back over the centuries, and on into the future, we find that Jesus taught us when he said, "I come not to destroy the Law, but to fulfill it."

Today we see how everything waits upon its own cause, and how change is only brought about by the processes of regular unfoldment. We know now that the Whole can only come into expression through the Part, and that the fulfillment of an individual, a nation, or a race must come under the silent operation of those spiritual laws of human understanding which neither the race nor the individual can outstrip.

God is law, and law began when life began and only a deep union with the finer relationships of Life can ever bring us into dominion of power.

There has ever been and ever will be many expressions of law, and between the Absolute expression and the finite results there must ever be the grinding to dust and ashes of things which oppose either the lesser or the larger unfoldment.

When we look at life from the limited, personal view we can only see from the boundary line of the unfathomed self; but as we come into deeper consciousness, we learn that expectation and promise built on personal hope is one thing, and expectation and promise built on universal understanding of universal action is another.

We are a part of everything in the universe and as we come to look through the personal to the universal, we see clearly the inseparable oneness of God-consciousness and man-consciousness, and as we understand and master this relationship, we can read the real answer to our question: "Where are the promises?"

Human life has always been, and always will be, only the unfolding of the personal mind into recognition of the Absolute Mind.

The Universe is under the Law Eternal and in the degree that we know this, we stop our limitations; mankind is free in the Absolute Law, and only seemingly bound in the finite one. Not one jot or tittle of the Law ever passes away; all laws exist to be fulfilled, but human life evolves from level to level of consciousness, and through relationship with higher understanding it escapes the primitive expressions of the lower laws and unites itself with the higher.

The very first truth, then, for any life to learn is, that in this universe of law and order, we get just what we relate with--no more, no less! Nothing happens; everything is the natural expression of the action which produces it.

Jesus came into the world under the law of his own life; he was born to pass along and die expressing the forms of his higher knowledge; he came and went under his own laws, but these were too obscure for the minds of that race to comprehend, and they lived, hoped and died, ignorant of his great Cosmic relationship. Jesus was a son of the planet and his mission was to set laws of race consciousness into activity which would act as a spiritual fulcrum throughout the ages.

What was true in these olden days is still true today; we often go on hoping that fulfillment will come, when by the very nature of what we are doing, we cannot get the higher expression. Take the simple things of our everyday life, our hope of health or our hope of love, wealth, place, happiness, success and usefulness; often we really do hope to be well, and plan in a way for that end, while really at the same time every breath we draw builds for the transitory and fleeting. Like the Christians of old we do not understand higher relationships, and at last, worn out with disappointment we cry, "Where are the promises?" and do not see that until we have perfect thought relationships, we cannot hope for perfect results. It takes deep perception to find the immutable law that all physical phenomena is mental arrangement.

We get everything we find expressing in life through the law of conscious or unconscious thinking! We have, and hold and keep only the things we create for ourselves; there is no other law; no one can take our own away; no one can give us anything, for only what we create is our own, and we alone must create it in consciousness before we can possess it. When we create it in consciousness we really set the law in operation for ourselves and this law will pass it into form.

We make our relationships through the thoughts of our mind. Our mind is the universal mind, and it is inseparably connected with everything in the universe; and whatever we have or have not is a signal of just what we have related with in consciousness. This is the unwritten action of the law; no one limits us but ourselves; the Universal Life stands ready with its many levels of relationships to give to every one according to the power he has to create for himself and he is really and truly judged "according to the deeds done in the body."

Jesus could not give an ignorant and undeveloped race the gift of a glorified kingdom; nor could they give it to themselves until they had related in consciousness with the laws that would produce it, the thing we want and our point of attraction must be equal.

We come into life under correct laws; one is not born a Jew, an Assyrian, an Englishman or an American by chance; nor is one born well and rich, and another sick and poor by chance, but each is the expression of the law with which he has related in his own consciousness.

Thoughts are things and it is a part of the Universal plan that thoughts from the human mind reach out into the Universal, or Cosmic mind, and there generate an energy which must in time embody in form and become the world picture of just what has been stimulated into expression. When thinking passes into a *fixed power* in our life it can be used to destroy or construct the body or the environment and every thought spoken or unspoken is registered in thought forms in our atmospheric environment and must some day pass into material form.

Health is the expression of a law brought about by a certain line of thinking and disease is another expression. Wealth is one law, poverty is another, and any life can choose this day *which* he wishes to be under, and choose this hour which law he will serve, and Jesus said, "Whomsoever ye yield yourself servants to obey, his servants ye are, whether it be sin unto death or salvation unto righteousness."

Jesus did not return to his disciples as they expected, because there was no Universal Law for such return. Just so with Health, Wealth, Love, Joy and Happiness. They can never come into expression for us so long as there is not established within us the Law of Natural Relationships.

We are learning at last that "Since the fathers fell asleep all things continue as they were from the creation," and it takes more than a fond imagination to pass our life from the law of inharmony, desire and pain, into the higher one of peace, power and happiness.

The moment a life desires anything it instantly becomes related with that thing, but it does not become a possession until all the conditions are fulfilled. Some minds think so *lightly* of everything that nothing ever becomes steadfast and certain. They drift aimlessly between loss and gain, health and disease, crying out, "Where are the promises," never realizing that promises are only fulfilled when the whole selfhood becomes grappled to the rock of understanding.

Human life is only a *growing* time, and each life will remain just where it is and express the laws of its level of consciousness until it develops out from them into others.

Sickness, poverty, wretchedness, disappointed hopes are common in the journey of Life; despairing human lives are common too, and lives full of rebellion can be found on every hand, but all these are the products of thoughts that produced them and show just where the consciousness has lingered.

Freedom from all these negative human experiences comes as the reward of inner growth; it can only come through unfoldment and transmutation into higher understanding. Human pain and loss, despair and disease, and the heart-breaks of life, are all the fruits of the Tree of Life whose root is *Truth*.

When sickness, sorrow and unhappiness have taken the place of health and joy in our life, we have no one to blame but ourselves; we can know that through a long line of perverted thinking, both inherited and acquired, we have become related with the laws in consciousness, and these laws are thoughts of self, hate, jealousy, strife, condemnation, resistance, etc. We have thought it unconsciously in the past, but until we stop and get up new thought relationships, these old things must go on. When we know the higher truth of New Thought Relationship, and the power of constructive thinking, we can begin then and there to change things and we instantly can clean out all the distorted thought energy, and pass the simple act of thinking into a creative form, quitting forever our response to the negative things around us.

We see the truth of "Whatsoever a man soweth, that also shall he reap," and we see, too, that this harvest field where we reap is the human life, and the seeds are thoughts, and we then and there fill our field of consciousness with thought-seeds of Health, Strength, Peace, Love, Joy and all the ten thousand beautiful constructive things, and we soon are living in a perfected thought world, surrounded by the dream pictures of our soul consciousness. We become like mystical seers, we can prophesy then about everything in our life without fear of contradiction, for knowing the Law that on the path "Like produces Like," and knowing the thought-seeds we sow, we can be certain of the future harvest.

Under the Law Eternal we cease to consider ourselves related to anything that we do not want. These things we do not want have ceased to exist for us, in the moment we have forgotten them in consciousness. We must refuse even to connect with them in memory. Sometimes this is a hard lesson: The Law of Memory is a peculiar force, it is the expression of fixed thinking--that which we cannot forget has made deep inroads into consciousness. Memory often keeps us related in strange ways, and hinders our unfoldment. Memory is the connecting link between the yesterday and today; it makes the past always the present and it remains the master of many lives and pours what it will into the field of consciousness until it is conquered.

We cannot go on to peace, power and divine unfoldment while we are wrapped around with olden memories, olden idols, fears and bondage.

It is an unwritten law that we pass on as we become fit, and any life can at any moment come away from the thought law of sin, sickness and death, into the law of peace, power, happiness and joy.

The great God-life wants us to have whatever we want, and will help us to get it and keep it. We have been told for ages to "ask and receive, seek and find, knock and it shall be opened." The Universal waits upon our recognition of its presence and before we ask it is given. The moment we know what we want and ask for it under the higher law of recognition, it is ours, then we only have to wait until we can manifest it. Over the same thought line which we pass out our desires, there passes back to us the answer to our prayers and our human pathway blossoms with the fruits and flowers of our deeper understanding.

The law of bondage will never become the law of liberty, but each one of us may come away into this perfect law of creative thinking as soon as we teach ourselves the simple act of picking out thoughts that relate us with the higher things of life. The kinds of positions, friends, conditions and environment we attract to ourselves under the positive conscious relationship are entirely different from the ones we will attract under the negative destructive thought laws. Good friends, happy environment, peace and love, are not made from the material of mind that recognizes only lack, loss, envy, despair, fear, condemnation and resistance.

When we want health, we must think health thoughts and become *one* with the laws that make for health and live at health's heights; when we want wealth we must create a wealth thought vibration and link our lives with the levels of wealth. All the grand, good things of earth can only come and gather around us when we have lifted our consciousness to the level at which they can be touched.

In the light of this higher understanding we can see that in just the proportion that our human nature rises towards the Universal Wisdom, our human perception becomes widened, until, at last, we include all the laws of higher living, thinking and being, and we bring from the hidden center within ourselves a profound knowledge. As our life grows more and more in the power of perception, we retire farther and farther from the personal, the pessimistic, the limited belief of selfishness, condemnation, resistance, and we begin a new thought life filled with moral, intellectual and spiritual glory, and even though "since the fathers fell asleep all things continue as they were from the creation," we see the true laws of creation, and making pur minds one with these laws we pass with them and through them on to perfected human wisdom, we turn to the daily life then with a higher, holier and more glorified purpose and out from all the gloom of the past we find the promises have all been answered and that God has provided some better things for us, which without us could not be made perfect.

The final word, then, to the sick, discouraged and diseased world is this:

"The righteous are in the hands of their God (the law) and their life is full of immortality," and knowing this anyone may recognize their conscious union with whatever they desire; create it in their human thought world and project it into form in the Cosmic Consciousness; then with wide open soul eyes walk calmly on, expecting it and never laying down their demand until it manifests for them.

The Outside And Inside Of Life

"Jesus said unto him, go and wash in the pool of Siloam. He went his way therefore and washed and came seeing." St. John IX, 7.

When we read the history of the ages behind us we cannot help but see that through every phase of human evolution there has run that subtle something which men call "the power of the unseen."

Matty of our forefathers lived in self scrutiny and subjective investigation, and many lived in lawless expression of their objective selves with no idea of life in its subjective action and form. As humanity advanced in its reverence it came to where lack of attention to regeneration and self-comprehension was followed by an inner sense of guilt, and those who know the power of the two states of consciousness, the outer and the inner, have grown to where they look upon it as abnormal to higher progress, to only enter these finer courts of being just to rest and renew the physical body.

Men instinctively know that life is too serious and mighty to pass along on the objective side of living without now and then going into the center of being and holding an earnest deep contact with the silent consciousness.

In the old thought world it was not strange for master men in every walk of life to pray. The powerful warrior turned his eyes from the field of battle to the strength of Heaven; the trusting mourner turned his eyes from the loss of earth to the gain of dying; even Milton gave himself to the discords of politics in action, and the symphonies of the seraphims. In the silence great lives everywhere have mingled the meditations of the Absolute with the thoughts of the discordant, differentiated and apparent *now*.

There is not a family anywhere that does not possess at least one person who in himself holds the proof of how real and earnest a thing are the exercises and consciousness of the solitary vigil.

There is something of reverence yet in many lives as they recall the blessing given at meals and the evening hour of prayer. To the wayward and those living in the control of the outside things of life, it was an hour of bondage, but to those who were at all awakened to the call of the inside life, it was an even-tide of peace and power and rest.

It cannot be denied that the years have brought great changes in the methods of human worship. The contempt with which some of the later educators treat worship and religion betray an ignorance on their part both of the true office of revelation and reverence, and this blinds them to the real, innate, fundamental longing of human life.

There are many who come away from the old thought and who believe in the promulgation of a new truth, but they attempt to build up the new through the destruction of the old, and pass along as Iconoclasts seeking what they can destroy. These lives are the lawful product of the undeveloped human comprehension, and the only safety for the race is in the fact that only a few ever take them seriously, and these soon see that they are not inclusive enough to help more than the few, and that after a while, in order to meet the demands of their own increasing individuality, they must themselves pass into wider union, into worship and get away from their own limitations.

Humanity must forever pass between the outside and the inside of life, and only as each soul becomes awake in both conditions can it understand and unite with the laws of perfect being.

New Thought is conscious of the open door between the inside and the outside of life, the earth and Heaven, and it knows that each soul may live from choice in either state of consciousness and pass in and out at will.

Man instinctively knows the difference between the inside and the outside of living; he can easily detect the laws of action, and the laws of silence. The tendency of our New Thought development is to teach lives to pass more and more into the inside power or, in other words, to come into the unseen laws of being and work consciously with the energy that creates and which is unmanifested, while at the same time they manipulate the manifested, external things, and through the understanding of the finite are able to bring into expression the absolute power.

It is slowly dawning upon the present day intelligence that through this inner side of mind we can become more and more capable of controlling and directing the outer states of human consciousness and men are recognizing more and more that all physical objective form is inner spiritual arrangement.

Today humanity is looking at the cant and form and creed of the crowd, and giving them their own rightful place, power and function, but it is also looking at the unseen and daring to affirm that an audience with God is attainable, certain and possible and productive of its own natural expressions in its own realm of higher recognition.

Today more than ever before new strength is being born into what the world calls the devotional element of humanity and it is being born on a sane, healthy plane of understanding which bids fair to revolutionize the world.

It does not take long to see, when we look with a clear vision, that those who display most power today, and who are productive of the greatest good to the developing world are not those who are living in fixed relationship with the outside of life; it is true that those on the outer rim may boast of perfect physical strength and a perfect brain and a physical beauty, but the victory today is not from the without, but it is rather for those who are psychologically practical, mystically enlightened and subtle with a deep scientific relationship with all nature's finer forces and who know life not alone as a science or as a philosophy, or as a religion, but as an art.

The truth must some day beat its way into the developing minds of men that we are now alive in a great age, and are coming to where the inside power must become externalized and that those who today stand masters of life, and those who will continue to become masters of life and leaders in power and helpfulness, must do it by a development that is not so much characterized by their objective knowledge as by their subjective holiness or wholeness.

We must learn what we never seem to have learned before, that the moments we spend in the external world are not wholly our strongest or sanest moments and that all external outside action is the crudest form of energy, and that when we want the *real*, we must turn the clear deep eye of our nature toward the inner, the silent, and then all our power seems to well up and meet us, because it is called in from the apparent to the Absolute of being.

The next great truth is that all the old ways of life are never thrown away until we have something to live by in the new; old truths never die, they are always existent, but their methods of expression must be changed to suit the developing intellectuality and spirituality of man.

In the old thought life prayer was the pathway to the interior world of power, but today we know that recognition must be the guide to the interior world of power. Prayer was the pathway of the old forefathers and prayer in its first inception was a straight road to the center of divine union, but after the minds of men, befogged between the glamour of the external and the power of the internal, evolved a form of prayer that led the race away from its center out into the rim of living, the power ceased; prayer became full of cant and form, words became meaningless and non-mystical; the truth that "God is a Spirit and they that worship Him must worship Him in spirit and in truth" was lost in the increasing bewilderment of the mind.

After a while humanity, seeing the futility of objective kind of prayer, ceased its praying, not because it had worn out prayer, not because it had wandered from its desire of worship and soul communion, but because it had worn out the old useless method, and found the dross of the letter; no one stood developed to where he could push faith into a new interpretation.

Self examination and supplication is natural to every life as soon as it develops to a finer knowledge of what passes within itself. Until the last man of the earth is dead this natural cry for the communion with the inner states of consciousness and the union with the great absolute God-life will rise up and flourish and wax strong in the souls of men.

We have learned now too much of the inside of living to ever be happy with the outside form alone, and we have seen too much of the unseen forces within us to ever yield ourselves servants completely to the external powers. Our spiritual analysis is too fine to permit crude interpretation. Men are leaving the old just as the seed must forever leave the mould and dust of earth, and push its stalk up into heaven's bright sunshine.

Today we stop and in close self questioning and with a desire to know the truth, and nothing but the truth, We ask what is it that has rendered the old thought piety of our fathers unnatural and impossible to us? It does not take long to answer this if we look with eyes that have clearer sight. Men have turned away simply because they were too developed to be fed on the husks of a worn out expression that was no longer large enough to satisfy their developing thirst for Truth.

Our New Thought methods have come because men built them with their desires; they called for methods that would fit the increasing spiritual comprehension of developing humanity.

Today mankind is instinctively recoiling from every sense of separation from God which our fathers felt; human life has become more human; the outside of life is known at its real value, the inside of life is given its place and power; Love has become vitalized; human affection has become sweet and natural; human duties are blessed privileges and life is elevated to a pinnacle of power before unknown; social interests are now beginning in all and ending in all; the whole scheme of man's natural moral and religious existence has a true worth and dignity of its own, and humanity is listening, accepting and delighting to honor and obey. Only the life in the outside ranks of living will ever condemn this new rise of power, and only the cowardly can despise; it is whole, sane, sweet and divinely human and humanly divine in its application and privileges.

We lost, perhaps, a great part of the old time manner of communion with God because we first lost the old time spirit of supplication and the groveling spirit of the outside world, but we have not lost communion or devotion.

Today we are at home in the center of being, and feel and know oneness. We have union now just as those who *know* truth have always had, but the method differs, and Silence has taken the place of the spoken prayer, meditation and silence is the new pathway to the Cosmic heart, and through this the developing children of men walk into perfect union, receiving the messages of the Divine Host. They come into a grand comradeship with God, not in the old time spirit of supplication and service, not asking, not seeking really, not even penitentially suppliant, but in the new found glory of a faith that looks up in perfect confidence of its oneness, and which speaks from the very depth of its own glorified selfhood, and knows that "I and my Father are *one* and all my Father hath is mine."

The new race will keep all that is vital in the old one of prayer and communion, and it will add to it all the great power of its own awakened consciousness. We are awake now--wide awake to the despotism of the outside world and its laws--and we are equally awake to the law of the inner side of life and the dominion of the world of pure Being.

Today the silence of our new understanding has become for developed humans the pathway of God, and it is indeed the pool of Siloam in which all may bathe and be healed.

The Silence becomes for those who seek it a well of living water that springs up into everlasting life.

It is promised that "the pure in heart shall see God," and anyone who comes away from the outside of life and comes stripped to the soul into the inner side of his own being will find God there, for like the vision of the monk, He is always there, waiting to be manifest.

The outside of life is beautiful and sweet and has in it many forms of self-realization; it is part of the plan of human development, but it is only a part and the lesser side of living, and after we have mastered its secrets and understood our own relationship to it, it is natural to turn inward, and read the other side of our life's picture, and when we do this it will be strange indeed if we do not feel the Eternal presence so close upon our soul that we will long to say with bated breath, "Thou God seest me."

The silence of the inner side of life and the power it produces cannot be put into words; it is the pathway to the Absolute and the *language* of *that* land is not spoken in the outer world of sense and sight.

Know the inner side of life, then *live* it--this is the pathway of peace and power and along this way there is found that strange vital, vibrant glow of spiritual illumination sanctifying our senses, and filling our soul and leading our mind into the fulness of Him who fills all.

Life then becomes for us a something divinely sent, no longer distraught; no longer to suffer; nothing but reality and a reality that has been known by millions throughout the ages and will be known by millions yet unborn.

Do not think that this turning into the inner side of living is weakness and cowardice and fear of the external world and its happenings; it is not, it is simply all energies united; it is not fear nor halting power, but it is rather the strength of the superhuman; it is not illusion, not self-hypnotism; it is a divine reality; it is God's witness to those who seek after his illuminated heights.

This living in the inner side of life each day is essential for the preservation of equalization of our daily life. The outside of life cannot help but become wearisome, and when we come away into the silence of our inner self, we find the thrill of life and we find the human made radiant with the glory of the Divine.

The inner side of life answers all the questionings of our mind, and as we learn this truth we depend less and less upon the things created, but live constantly in the energy that creates, and through this operate our whole life.

Silence was first in the scheme of creation. Remember this: "The darkness and the silence knew. So is a man's fate born."

There is no creation that will last that is born on the plane of external action for the law of that plane is change. In the hush of the valley of silence we accumulate the inward power which pushes our external expression into bloom. In the inner side of living the soul enlarges its dimensions and when it comes back into the earthly things it gilds them with a glory not their own.

The inner side of life and its power is not a mysterious thing, it is only the finding of God, and when we meet Him face to face, we speak in a new tongue; we live in a temple not made by hands, eternal in the heavens, and we live in the truth of the olden mystics and say with the power of our new consciousness: "Our Father, hallowed be Thy name, Thy kingdom has come, Thy will is done on earth, as it is in Heaven."

The Measure Of Ourself

"And he that talked with me had a golden reed to measure the city, and the gates thereof and the wall thereof. And the length and the breadth and the height are equal."

The building of a glorious perfected selfhood, this is the work of every life.

We all come into existence equal in privilege, we are all born equal in latent power, which, if developed, will keep us shoulder to shoulder in this game of living out; but not until this latent power is developed and brought out into external manifestation can any life really declare its mastery.

Life has one grand prize for all, and this prize is life's master position. The chance to compete for this prize is given to all at birth, but the power to push forward in the pursuit of it is only developed by those who know that it is really within them, and knowing this begin systematically to unfold it. Not everyone is equal in the externalization of this latent energy, and no matter how much or how little any life may possess it, still it has its own point of contact for power, and it can come forth in its own way in wisdom of conquest.

Life as we find it here on earth is like a great garden; each soul comes into this world garden and its place and keynote is struck upon the harp of life and the registration is made in the universal harmony; then it must work out its own part until it comes into perfect tune with the other parts of the great universal chord.

Not a life is born into expression here, but in the unseen realm an angel or higher master ministers at its birth, and its name is written in the Lamb's book of life (or the Universal Cosmic Mind). Each life drops into its own selected and appointed place; it has its own special mission to perform, its own lessons to learn, its own part to work out, and its own grand privilege of development.

In essence all life is *one*, and all humanity is the same; the *One Life* is in all and through all, without regard to class, creed or color, but in manifested expression we must forever be different; some lives are younger in their unfoldment--they are unfinished; some have finer bodies through which to manifest consciousness; some are born into positions where there is more required of them than of others, for the price of usefulness is the ability to be useful; some are never useful and live idle aimless lives because they have not yet incorporated within themselves the power to be of use to others.

The nation, the race, the individual and the environment are simply signals which we hang upon ourself of just what we created and unfolded within our own consciousness.

We come the reaper of the things we sowed, and just where we find ourselves here is the picture of how well or how ill we have used the years behind us, but the privilege of new use and new development is still within us; we stand each day on the threshold of a new lifetime, ready to begin over and over again our new unfoldment.

Around each life is the *All Consciousness*, and it can fashion for itself a new world, made of the cosmic substance with which it is connected.

The great unfolding mass of humanity pass along, taking themselves as a confused bundle of states of being, acted upon by the external force of people and environment, and in turn acting back with no conscious idea of creation, never knowing that with what measure we mete it shall be meted unto us.

This process of being acted upon and acting back unconsciously, produces a type of energy that cannot fail but bring forth masses of individuals who are in bondage, body, mind and spirit, for spirit has not sensed its eternal birthright of liberty.

Looking at this world garden full of natural wild flowers, called the "human race," New Thought sees clearly that whatever response an individual gives to his environment is the evidence of his own special power, and that this personal power may, by conscious control and direction, give him complete mastery, and through this he passes uninterrupted into possession of life's master position and the prize of peace and power and wisdom.

The individual is always the actor; the environment is always acted upon, and this acting and acting upon again gives forth an expression, and the exchange and inter-exchange between the two produces what the world calls the character of a life, and looking upon the product of this play of forces, we say "he is a genius," "he is a thief," "he is a God-man," or, "he is a degenerate," measuring with the example that is hung before our eyes.

Up to this point all men are really equal; they are simply alive in consciousness, but just as the gardener takes the flower and transplants it to specialized soil, and causes it to bud and bloom with all the energy within it, just so man's own consciousness can take his soul and teach him how he can lift himself into states of specialized human power and show forth all the glory of a divinely developed man.

Everyone can take his place at any level of living that he chooses just as soon as he knows that there is no one to say "no" to him but himself.

Strong positive thoughts put truth into the hearts of men, and this builds them upward and inward towards harmony.

This great universal law of harmonious consciousness is the reed with which everyone may measure himself and with which each one is taught to take his own dimensions and never lay it down until his city of character stands equal in height, breadth, and depth, and length.

When we measure ourselves by the golden reed of consciousness, we find by the signs of ourself and our environment if our city of self is right, and if it is not we can rebuild it in finer architectural fashioning.

There are many lives that have neither breadth, nor height, nor depth, they have only length; they pass along through life tied to one idea or at least a few ideas; they are narrow, bigoted, selfish and careless about the other dimensions of themselves; they see through their glass darkly, the things of their own immediate knowledge are enough for them; they are exclusive and powerful in one direction, and humanity might break itself to pieces just outside their narrow life for they neither hear nor care; they are all right, secure in their length of narrow, personal endeavor. They are afraid of anything that is outside of their own field of vision, and their life is altogether too small and straight and strained, for any but a few of their own kind to hold on to; their days are full of anxiety and worry, for their hold on truth is too weak to bring them to power, and wisdom.

Again, after we see how we measure in length, we can turn the golden reed upon ourselves for specialization in breadth, and often again we find a shortcoming. The breadth must also be equal; we cannot fail in our breadth and come into true wisdom, true breadth means inclusion--this may vary in degree, but there must never be exclusion of anything in the well-rounded character, there is conscious selection, but never exclusion; there is nothing *in* or *under* or *above* the earth but that is companion with us on our journey toward divine unfoldment.

To make the breadth of our life measure up in fulness, we must look with wide open eyes at everything and everyone in life, and take it at its own point of unfoldment. Not in every life is found true wisdom of thought and expression, but if we know the truth we will see past all the undeveloped things within, to the beautiful God-self it is becoming and with wisdom and power and love include it in our own consciousness, waiting patiently for its development.

To have breadth we must open our ears and our life to the call of the world voice and live to answer it. We must hear it socially, ethically, individually, financially, politically, religiously, spiritually, mentally and physically not only in our own way, but in every way can that one find God within himself before he can find it through humanity; but when measured by the golden reed for the building of the new self, we must find God or Good in and through every living creature.

All people love themselves and most people love their own families; and this is right and good that it is so, but the breadth and height and depth must be equal and that means inclusion of the universal as well as the personal self. Jesus again told this when he said to the man who asked him "What shall I do that I may have eternal life?" And He said unto him: "Keep the commandments" and, "Thou shalt not bear false witness:" "And the young man saith unto Him, 'All these things have I kept from my youth up; what lack I yet?'" "Jesus saith unto him: 'If thou wilt be perfect, go and sell all that thou hast and give to the poor, and thou shalt have treasure in Heaven and come and follow me.' But when the young man heard that saying, he went away sorrowful, for he had great possessions." So when Jesus measured him by the reed of breadth and deeper inclusion, he followed him no more, for the height, the breadth and the depth were not equal.

To give to ourselves and to our own, or to those who seem to have a claim on us for anything, is good, but, to give to those who have not claim or kinship nor power over us is *greatness*. To include them in our own world, not by might or force, but through recognition of union with the one life-- this is consciousness of breadth that remains immortal.

Again, the depth of a life must be equal, and how do we lack in this? There are thousands today who flit along on the crest of the wave of life's current, butterfly-like; they never really have a conscious thought. If "it only does not affect me" is their watchword, and freedom from anything serious is their only really serious problem. They know in an indifferent way that hearts break, that tears fall, that there are prayers that stagger upward through life's storm, but the froth and foam of life is in their eyes; they look out on the rim of a life where they see only self-indulgence, and when now and then they are hushed long enough to listen to the world cry, they turn away quickly for fear they will actually touch lives with the common people.

So long as they keep afloat they are content, their lack of depth does not disturb them, but often after they have wasted their all in riotous living, and the realities of life fall upon them, they cry out from the depth of their own self-made despair; their life was like a palace built on sand which the first fierce flood tide could destroy; it had no root, no place in consciousness when measured by the golden reed--the height, the breadth and the depth were unequal.

Unless the soul has root in soil divine, it cannot face earth's overwhelming expressions of the working out of the human laws which it sets in motion in the round of human living.

The life that would build sublime and lasting things to stand the test of time, must drop its consciousness into the Absolute, and sink the string of thought into the fathomless!

Lights and shadows are strangely blended all along the human pathway; so from the very center of the deeps of life the incense of our illumined selves must still send up a faint sweet breath outward and onward,--then the breadth as touched by the golden reed is equal.

Again, the height of the perfect self is also measured. No house so low but it must have a window opening to the sky.

Again, there are many lives that touch the golden reed as it measures outward, downward, but are insensible of upward power.

Above the surge and din of life, amid its sorrows and its strife, the soul that comes under the glory of the golden reed, must lift itself to the hills of specialized wisdom greater then the common consciousness.

We can find many noble, moral, natural lives equal in length and breadth and depth, but the height is lacking. Within many minds is lack of great sublime ideals, ideals that should be born in the illumined centers of the self. There are many who have no communion with their source; they are kind, sociable, natural, humanitarian, but lacking in that great wonderful psychological essence which makes the human half divine; the height of their life is unfinished, the golden reed is broken; they walk on superior in their knowledge until in some supreme hour of human grief, their soul is forced through some Gethsemane and opens its eyes to the need of a strength beyond their own. Death, the grave and love teach them to look up, and hope higher than the earthly kingdom.

And once more the measure of our soul goes on, and we find that often all is equal, but the height is *over-reached*; there are many forgetting breadth and length and depth who measure into the very hill-tops of illumination, making their whole expression a dream of no value to themselves or others. They are pure children of spirit; they live in a world peopled with the dream-children of their mind and everything they produce is vapid and useless in the world in which they live and have being; everything seems to pass away from them and their productions are as nothing under the crush and strain of life around.

Use is the world's great test of anything; unless it can be utilized by some one it is valueless to aid humanity; everything that comes forth into form from any state of consciousness must prove its own power to persist, or it vanishes and is forgotten.

Nothing too high, nothing too low, nothing too wide, nothing too narrow, too shallow, but all perfectly adjusted--this is the measure of self, and when we know this the illumined life works out its own unfoldment, passing at will to any degree of consciousness.

This is the finished product of the life that knows how to specialize in consciousness and it is made possible through deeper illumination. It gives to everyone the glorious physical, a depth of perception, radiant with a refined energy and alive with all the latent power of instinct and harmony, and with this the brilliant mind with its breadth of unanswerable logic, its fine facts, science of order and laws of physical adjustment. And added to both these we find the dream vision of the psychic, with the poet's soul of inspiration, sublime ideality and the gentle tender heart, alive with all the common human emotions; and at last, blended and transmuted and made vibrant by that great spiritual insight born on the heights of human revelation we find ourselves whole, grand, developed, humanly divine creatures, walking in glad comradeship with God.

This is the "Holy Grail" of selfhood and in the light of our higher understanding we look downward and outward and upward, and the length and the breadth and the height are equal. We pass from the old race thought of limitation and live in a divine atmosphere, and can say with a wisdom born from this fuller comprehension:

"We know that if our house of this earthly tabernacle were dissolved, we have a building of God--an house not made with hands, Eternal in the heavens."

Perfect Liberty

"No man liveth to himself and no man dieth to himself."

The more we look at humanity and study its expressions, the more we become convinced of the truth of these words. It is not hard to see that our human ties are closely knit with everything and everyone, but it is not always easy to understand how they have come to their sometimes almost hopeless tangle.

We are a part of everything in the universe, seen and unseen, and as we have within us a response to every emotion, hope dream, impulse of any kind known or recognized by the human race. As we study and understand our relationship to people, things and expressions, we cannot help but grow deeper and deeper into the clearness of the great truth, namely, the universal and abiding one-ness of man and God.

Some of our relationships in this one-ness are very indistinct and obscure, while some are very distinct and painfully objectified.

The first Truth for us to take up is this--we *have* and *express* in our being and our environment just these things with which we have related ourselves, either through inherited or acquired lines of thinking; no one gives to us but ourselves, no one takes away from us but ourselves, no one is to blame but ourselves whatever we have or have not; we, and we alone, are the architects of our own fortune or misfortune.

We get everything in life by the law of conscious or unconscious relationship with it through the simple act of thinking; our thoughts are lines of transference over which may pass to us not only the things which we desire, but also those which our fear brings down upon us and which we do not desire.

Unconscious relationship differs from conscious relationship and brings us the things with which we have connected through the law of omission; conscious relationship is union, and brings everything into expression under the law of commission.

Both of these lines are constant and their results undeniable, but one brings us the whole, the constructive, while the other opens our life for the control of the destructive, the limited.

When thinking passes into a fixed power in our life, it may be used to perfect or destroy the whole mechanism of our present and our future. Long lines of conscious and unconscious thinking bring about certain expressions, and these expressions in time become a part of our very existence, and our environment, good or bad, bears witness to this relationship.

One day upon the streets of Boston I saw an old woman selling newspapers; her hair was gray, her skin brown and wrinkled, her clothing shabby and only half sufficient for the chill of the hour; she was simply poverty-stricken, and her old, thin, piping voice trembled as she called her papers in an effort to compete with the crowds of newsboys around her. Many bought her papers, drawn to her through pity, and her evident need. I felt sorry that with her gray hair so near the grave life should have only this to offer her, and I sought a reason for it. I asked her to tell her story.

She was the daughter of a minister; her mother had been the proverbially meek little woman of history, perfectly fitted to be her father's wife. Her grandfathers on both sides of the parental tree had been ministers; she gave me a graphic sketch of the long line of concentration which she had been born into and in which she continued.

There was a long line for concentration and relationship with lowliness of spirit, for grace, for the utter sinking of self; lack of demand for place or power; lack of self-righteousness, absolute submission sown through generations, sown for her in her own life. It had to bring forth its fruit and it did bring it forth in the form of that gray-haired, beautiful, ragged old woman, who, in the days of her declining years, gathered her harvest on the cold streets of a rich city, underfed, poor and alone.

She was still true to her inherited concentration, for while I questioned her she said, "Health, money and happiness were not for her," and that "her family had borne the cross of poverty and sickness all their lives and borne it nobly, and some day the Father would give them their reward." Don't you see that the mind that is poised where her mind was, and where her family's mind had been for generations, could not escape the law which they had built for themselves.

Here was an example of unconscious relationship; can't you see how unwittingly she hourly and daily made anew her relations with the very things which must by their very nature divorce her from the things which she never sensed belonged to her. The fixed thinking handed down to her from the past, bound her like a galley-slave and kept her life held against the law which was daily destroying her; she was unconsciously related and she remained unconsciously related to the laws which made for loss and lack in her life, unable to see the paths where she turned aside from her Father's house, and His universal abundance; blind to her power of new creating.

When we begin to study our lines of unconscious relationship we find that we are appalled almost at the ten thousand little tendrils which bind us to our old relationships; we think ourselves "good easy man" this moment, and the next moment sees us opening the door of our life to thought forms which if entertained, will certainly become for us a poor relation, and demand our support for ages. We daily open our lives to endless tramp thoughts which dwell with us and in the end beggar us.

We need hourly to set a guard on our field of unconsciousness, and absolutely refuse to admit into our daily mind any thoughts less than those which distinctly relate us with all the beautiful things of life, and we must never forget the truth of the power of our own personal creations. We can be what we *will* to be; we can be related to whatever we choose to be related to; we can choose this day whom we will serve and start the hour of our rebuilding.

Whatever we have or have not is a positive picture of our relationship and tells to every passer-by the story of just how well we know how to control, and direct our own thoughts, and whether we are living unconsciously or consciously.

The way to get the Perfect Liberty for ourselves is to understand fully the secret of relating ourselves with it through the power of conscious thinking.

The moment that a life desires anything, be it health, wealth or love, it becomes related with that thing, and the thought establishes a line of direct transference; desire is the first out-reaching for the things which are necessary to fully develop our life. It is the God-push within us trying to get our consciousness into expression.

In the past, the educators often called this power of conscious relationship, "persistency"; have you not seen people whom the world called "hobby riders" or "freaks"? These people are only perverted in the expression of conscious relationship; they hold their relationship to one thing to the exclusion of every other thing in their life.

It is just as much a form of misdirected energy to sink everything in life to one idea; to sacrifice health, friends, position, peace, everything, in order to gain one thing, as it is to have a diverse, indefinite, faltering idea of relationships and purposes. The true position is between them: All things work together for the final good of man, and union with *all* things, not *one* thing, is the law of *universal* development.

Once we have decided what we want to be related with we can afford to let everything take its own appointed time and place in our life, bringing everything up in its appointed place. All that we have to do is to keep our fixed point of attachment with it and this attachment is made through power thoughts.

Substance is always changing and so is our position to it under the common law, but under the conscious law of creation we change our position over and over again, but we keep the same hope until in some expected hour we stand face to face with our hope manifested in form.

There is no use running after anything; no use straining after it! We gain liberty not by resistance, denial or renunciation, but through union; under the old law we worked on the plane of competition; in the perfected imaging or thinking we are living under the law of divine attraction, and whatever we relate ourselves with in thought must come and join us.

When we are under this law thousands of unseen hands reach out to lift us into peace-crowned heights, and into relation with what we desire.

When sickness has taken the place of health in our life, when disease has crowded out our ease and comfort, we can know that by a long line of perverted thinking, perhaps both inherited and acquired, we have become related with those things which are under the law of pain, destruction and disintegration. We may have done all this thinking unconsciously in the past, but there is now no excuse for us to go on with this old relationship; it is senseless to again fill up our field of consciousness with the old thought concepts.

When we know the truth of this transference into form through thought relationship, we have perfect liberty; we look at ourselves in a new light, and begin to then and there pass this simple act of thinking into lines which will connect us with just these things which we desire; we quit forever our thought relationship with conditions which speak for lack or loss or limitations.

We fill our field of consciousness with thoughts of the strong, and the health of life; we shut out the diseased, the dwarfed, the imperfect. We force the pictures of hospitals and sanatoriums out of our mind; we look at our bodies no matter how they look, or how much of disease they are then expressing, and we see only the *whole*, the new, the complete. We force ourselves to *know* nothing but the great all health thoughts; we go back again and again to our relation with the abundance of health; we make ourselves deaf and blind and dumb to the absence of wholeness and our body slowly swings into line, and begins to express for us the nature of our conscious thinking.

We cease to consider ourselves related to anything that we do not want. Disease, pain, lack of health may have its place in the lesser relationships of the human plane, but it is not found in the kingdom of consciousness--the all-health within us; it cannot exist in this new world of spiritual chemicalization with which we have taken up our relations.

When we want this perfect law of liberty, we do not recognize the existence of the old, we simply occupy our whole thought time with the new things with which we wish to make union.

Every condition of life that we consider desirable for ourselves we convince ourselves is already ours, we reach out and lay hold of it, and give it a line of transference into our life. This is not castle building, this is Divine Relationship--the Perfect Law of Liberty!

We see the truth that the strong, the healthy, the happy, the powerful are living in the same world, in the same universal energy that obtains for the diseased, the weak, the sick, the unhappy; there is no reason why they may not have every good and perfect gift.

There are almost as many healthy as there are sick in every hospital--the doctors, nurses, porters, cooks, and servants, all hale and hearty, putting in their whole time caring for those who are half dead with disease. What makes the difference? Just the difference of relationship. They have not accepted mentally the same conditions, and even surrounded as they are with the sick and diseased, they refuse to be bound by the laws which these patients have endowed with power over themselves.

They have learned the two great truths: There is nothing in all the world that has any power over us except that with which we endow it, and there is nothing in all the world of which we need be afraid. Disease and sickness are signals of great negative conditions of mind which we have recognized in thought, and exalted to the *king* chair in our life and endowed with power to hold us in bondage.

We may escape in just that hour that we sense the power of our own personal creation, and set up a conscious relationship with the positive constructive things in our own consciousness. We become lords of our physical conditions and our environment just as soon as we cut out all thought relationship with the laws which make for loss and lack. "The spirit beareth witness with our spirit day by day that we are the Sons of God," and as soon as the soul knows this it senses its divine relationship, and is born again on the planes of a higher consciousness, and in the wisdom of its understanding it builds itself new conditions, and lives in a new world, surrounded with the objects of its own creating, at first subjectively, but in time manifested on the objective plane, to bear witness to the truth which its soul knows and obeys.

When this is done we live in a new world made perfect by our own inspired workmanship; we know nothing of disease and pain, we have never a morrow of fear, "our today of content is eternal."

There are many who have mastered health, because it was the first thing they demanded, and after they have done this, they find that they are still related to the laws which make for poverty and lack in material possessions; they have liberty in flesh but not the perfect law of it in environment. There are those who have known the grinding hand of need, who have stood with crushed lives, hopeless; with courage dead and the devil of despair crouched on their shoulder, whispering words of disappointment; there are those who are homeless in a land of homes, and those who are starving in a world of plenty; what can we say to them? How can we comfort them and point them to the hope of a new endeavor?

The world is full of these half-fledged lives and we must answer them. In order to meet this expression we must go back again to our first truth, our first statement:--"We *have* and *express* in our being and our environment just these things with which we have related ourselves, either through inherited or acquired lines of thinking; no one gives to us but ourselves, no one takes away from us but ourselves, no one is to blame but ourselves whatever we have or have not; we, and we alone, are the architects of our own fortune or misfortune."

As soon as we can teach a life to know the truth of its own power of conscious thought relationship, it can face about and begin a new line of attraction and accumulation. It is an unwritten law that we pass on as we become fit, and we can at any moment begin a new thought attitude which, if persisted in, will relate us with everything which we conceive to be opulence or abundance.

When we want to come into perfect liberty for wealth, we must never recognize poverty or the things which make for it; we must refuse to sense a separation from whatever we desire; the universal abundance is for all, and we get and express just the amount we have power to connect.

The all will wants us to have whatever we want, remember this! And it will aid us to secure what we want and help us to keep it just so long as we show we can make intelligent connection with it.

We must believe in our divine kinship with supply, and the divine kinship of every other soul with it; over the same line which we send out our desire for abundance there will pass back to us the answer to our prayer;

the things we seek are seeking us; this is a great psychological truth which we can prove to ourselves if we try. Under the lines of the higher spiritual affinity the lines of transference never cross; our gain never becomes another's loss, and *vice versa*.

The whole scheme of life is for freedom; it is only the perverted building of the minds of men that have externalized lack and bondage. We have forgotten the eternal promise, "With what measure ye mete it shall be meted unto you," we have related with lack of supply, never knowing the truth that no one limits us but ourselves.

Under the law of liberty, we place ourselves in the very heart of divine opulence and though at first we cry abundance from the very depth of poverty, if we hold our life servant to this relation, all lack will slowly slip away from us, and we can, and *do* walk out into new relations of attraction, and become one with all that our Father hath.

This, then, is the truth of perfect liberty:

"To him that hath shall be given, and from him that hath not shall be taken away even that which he hath."

Those who have laid hold of the Divine truth of abundance of supply and related themselves with it through the power of conscious thinking may go on in calm security from demand to supply, coming each day deeper into the universal cosmic opulence of health, wealth, love and usefulness.

The word, then, to the sick or poverty-stricken or loveless is this: Recognize your union with whatever you desire; reach out and make relation with it through the power of conscious thinking; look with wide open soul eyes straight into the face of the Universal Being, and taking your wants firmly into your mind walk on in your daily life demanding them and expecting them to manifest; never lay down your consecration until it does express for you.

Make every conscious relationship one with health, wealth, love and usefulness, accompanied by peace, power, plenty and divine realization.

As soon as we lift our personal life to the level of the universal life in positive recognition of our own, it will come to us and abide.

Union with the cosmic life is a possible thing here and now; the human life is but the remote picture of our place in the universal; our life's relations may become the flowers on our tree of life, and our manifold experiences the fruits of our own growing and all life be one perfect round of liberty born from conscious righteous choice.

Cosmic Therapeutics

"And He stood between the living and the dead, and the plague was stayed."

The greatest secret of the age is the connection with and manipulation of the cosmic energy.

In every age and every race men have stumbled on to relationship with their atmospheric environment and have each demonstrated it in their own way, but it remained for the twentieth century investigators to give us the real key to our continuous connection and the methods by which this connection could be demonstrated to the thinking world.

The minds of the past taught us the existence of an atmospheric environment and to a degree manifested our connection with it, but accomplished it through the medium of objective lines of connection and transference; today we are finding the new truth that man is able to create his own environment even to the most minute thing and create it from atmospheric energy lifting his creations aloft in his life in finite form through the medium of a power that, in its first expression, far transcends sight and touch.

Today we know that the great Cosmic currents in which the whole world lives, and moves, is nothing but a vast undifferentiated sea of energy. This energy is acting always in the formless as electrical currents; these currents are always waiting to be set in motion with any other current which corresponds with them in electrical reaction either positive or negative.

Man's whole atmospheric environment is formed of these currents and he is a localized attracting center, registering in himself and his environment just those electrical reactions with which he relates under the great Cosmic law of correspondence.

We have found in the past that these atmospheric currents can be sent as vibrations through the medium of any object that is brought into relation with them and the degree of registration depends upon the instrument used.

In some rates of vibration these waves may be made to become heat; in others, cold; in others, light; in others, sound; in others, just motion, without sound being separated. Physical science has given us examples too numerous to mention of the positive expression of enforced vibration in relation to objective things, but it was left for Marconi to show conclusively that these vibrations may be produced and transmitted through the medium of the atmospheric waves themselves, and psychology has shown that any instrument, either mechanical or human, may register vibrations in the very moment they are attuned to them.

Atmospheric environment has passed deeply into the development stage scientifically, and even in this it does not yet really appear what it may be, but it is easy to see how all atmospheric energy becomes really a substance from which every skilled mechanic may create his own expression.

Metaphysically, it is plain to see that man is only one part of this great cosmic energy, and that standing as he does, a localized point in the ocean of formless vibrating ether, he becomes a specialized, attracting center and the lines which connect him with this ocean of energy are his own thoughts.

In the physical plane men use wires and machines and objective localization, but on the higher planes of consciousness we only need to use the vibrations of that plane, and the higher connecting thought wires become as tangible to those who use them as do the objective connections on the physical planes.

On the human plane our thoughts become the metaphysical avenues of connection; with thoughts we reach out into this formless ocean of cosmic energy and create through recognition the things which we desire, and our environment under this law becomes the world-picture of just what we have had the power to create for ourselves.

This cosmic substance is neither great, nor small, finite nor infinite, it simply is substance from the highest to the lowest expression of life. There is no escaping this universal product of energy. We ourselves are It!

The physical universe, and everything that we call matter, is simply *universal energy* manifested in form; everything expressed on the physical plane is cosmic energy materialized; and every human being is only this cosmic energy localized and expressed in human flesh and form. Form is only the physical side of Divine mind.

In this ocean of universal energy or atmospheric environment which we call formless, there is always some form of some kind, but the formless is a form too high for our human mind to comprehend, we have not yet reached the plane of unfoldment where we have cosmic recognition.

As we investigate this atmospheric environment, we find it has two distinct forces at work within it, and these forces are the positive and negative reaction of its atoms. This positive and negative reaction of the atoms is continually going on, and they each have their corresponding embodiment in the eternal world of matter; they act independently or together, and when one has learned how to blend these two reactions in his consciousness, as do the skilled magi, he has come to the center of his own and universal being.

In the manifested world of substance, mankind takes its place in one or both of these energies; it is drawn into their expression by the universal law of attraction. Each life is in its first expression, positive or negative in its cosmic polarity. In the universal interpretation, we learn to look upon the positive life as the creative, and the negative life as the receptive.

Every individual is just what he is by the natural law of his own cosmic relationship, and he will remain just what he is at any point of progress, and express himself in his own way until he grows into a deeper state of comprehension, and knows the method of changing his cosmic positions.

When we get the truth of the universal energy in our minds and realize that this energy is really positive and negative, and that both these reactions have their corresponding material manifestation in ourselves, then we are ready to go farther into the study of the registration of this energy, and from this into the higher psychology of function.

There is nothing in this atmospheric environment of ours that is not endowed with intelligence. Everyone who postulates a *first cause* begins with the universal *intelligence*. This *intelligence* is given to us as a beginning, it remains with us to the end.

The acceptation of the truth of the unity of intelligence is the first step toward investigation. All finite life is an embodiment of universal substance and intelligence in some form--this is truth.

Physical scientists everywhere are showing us the infinitesimal lives working continually and in ways that are wonderful.

Psychologists are opening daily the hidden chambers of this physical and metaphysical world, and giving us high lights on what we once thought impossible of investigation; they are showing us astounding examples of conscious ideation in every order of life, and are aiding us to draw interesting conclusions.

There is a great universal intelligence and a remote finite expression of this intelligence; the lesser is always dependent upon the greater and our human life becomes the microcosmic pattern of the macrocosmic world.

With this premise firmly under our feet let us go on to the question of the intelligence of the physical tissues of the human body, and our relation to disease, health, poverty and opulence.

Every cell of our physical body is intelligent and capable of being instructed into finer grades of expression; this is the process by which we refine matter into spirit and by which we pass from a lower to a higher expression of wholeness and build our cells into a grade of consciousness so high that we produce objective expressions of such perfect response that we become the higher revelation of the cosmic consciousness.

The higher we go in intellectualizing ourselves, the closer we draw to the cosmic consciousness, and the more familiar we become with its laws. The highest life is the one that includes the most.

It is a natural law that we have at all times unconscious thought relation to the universal abundance and our thoughts are the conscious agents of construction and destruction, and we work through them as soon as we are old enough to think and reason.

Disease and poverty would never manifest for us if we did not some time recognize it in our atmospheric environment with our thoughts, and work it out on the objective plane through the law of atomic attraction.

Whenever doubt, worry, anger and negative thoughts take possession of our field of consciousness (the everyday mind), we are creating these things for ourselves in the cosmic currents and they cannot refuse to register in form either in our body or in our environment.

It can be seen that if, year after year, we separate ourselves from the positive creative cosmic intelligence, and put up our images of personal limitation, the creative intelligence is joined to the weaker energy and cannot refuse to work out the conditions with which they are related.

The human mind is the agent which must be taught to stand as sentinel and force our minds to people our currents with thoughts which make only for the perfect health, perpetual opulence and divine realizations.

The minor intelligence of our cells would just as readily work out the universal law of perfection if we only knew enough to intelligently direct them and not overpower them by our negative personal directions.

When we have once established in our minds the truth of this universal cosmic intelligence, in which there is no sickness, poverty or death, unless we recognize it, it does not take us long to work out better conditions for ourselves in the physical body and environment.

No matter what our lack may be, we can know that it is because we have set our human thought to work under a personal negative law instead of a positive creative universal one. We have only to stop, face about, and begin to direct our thoughts intelligently, and in union with the higher plan, and solicit co-operation with all the finite forces around us.

If we find ourselves diseased, with pain, and physical mal-positions we can speak to our physical cells as we would to a friend and connect them with the higher creative currents and help them to get into a higher form of building; they are ready at any moment to answer, "The sheep know their shepherd's voice and obey it." They must begin to build in the new likeness and in the very moment that we consciously direct them; this is the law, there is no appeal from it.

Everything comes to us from the Infinite atomic ethers through the law of Divine attraction, and when we have built and rebuilt our cells into an intelligent relationship with absolute wholeness, we become a magnet, so highly sensitized and so magnetic and carefully polarized, that we are an attracting center for everything in our atmospheric environment, and our physical body and our environment become the expression of our thought world.

When we know enough to send our thoughts into the universal energy with only the recognitions of positive creations, such as health, wealth, love, divine realization and actualization, then our material world must be made the immediate reproduction of these things.

The sick world passes along with all its thoughts poised in the destructive recognition; we meet them upon this pathway, and knowing the law of the higher constructive power of building we must meet their questioning with some answer that will restore them to the state of consciousness they have lost.

The very first truth that every sick life must know is that thoughts are *things*, and make themselves felt in form, and that in the great atmospheric energy, like attracts like. Our consciousness becomes for us the wireless stations which attract and register the universal messages, and each station attracts its own from whatever plane or state of consciousness it vibrates.

The invisible world is *something* and its substance is *something*, and that we do not understand it and have improper correspondence, is no proof that the power of correct correspondence does not exist.

There are great occult laws of relationship always awaiting our deepening comprehension:

> *"Till one appears who bears,*
> *All nature silent is,*
> *Silent for evermore,*
> *Beating its waves of force*

On an unanswering shore
Till one appears who bears."

The cosmic atmospheric energy in which we live, move and have our being is always ready to become manifested in form, and may become manifested by anyone who knows how to create a form for himself.

It has been manifested in many varied forms by the children of men, but it has not yet entered into the hearts of men to conceive of the glories that are yet awaiting them when one appears who really does hear, and knows the full truths of cosmic power.

This is the secret of Cosmic Therapeutics, and those who know this secret really do become the twentieth century mystics and are rulers over the manifestations of finite and infinite energy. When we come to this point of demonstration we are the world's greatest physicians. With this knowledge we may conquer not only disease and poverty and despair, but we may overcome the last enemy--Death, and live and have being in a world of universal power.

There are grades and grades of intelligence both in the human and the Absolute mind: All grades of cosmic currents are ever ready waiting to respond to those who touch them; there is nothing mysterious or unattainable about them; they are the natural results of natural laws, and we come into union with them through growth and recognition.

We first come to a consciousness of our universal, atmospheric relationship with all that is, then we learn to understand the response that comes to us from every person and everything; then we reach out in perfect faith with our deep of need, calling to the deep of supply, and the doors of a thousand hidden chambers of nature open bringing divine revelation into our souls.

Absent Treatments

The sick world has always had its scientific and religious investigation, and in addition to this new-found power of atmospheric creation there is another great truth which the sick world must know in order to make its own union, and this is the truth of the power to manipulate these Cosmic currents not only of our own creation, but for anyone who touches our life; we cannot only think and realize and actualize for ourselves, but we can reach out into the formless energy and create, direct and control these great universal currents so that they will have the power to rebuild another's life.

We have a great psychological Cosmic truth known as "absent treatments" but which is really cosmic therapeutics in our new understanding; we use cosmic currents to heal ourselves and we manipulate them for another thereby eliminating time and distance; we get behind the things created and understand and deal with the Energy which creates.

The sick world has tried all the things of the physical world through the medium of objective lines of transference--drugs, electricity, diet, baths and what not, each one a part of the cosmic consciousness, but it finds that the laws still exist, and as long as they remain related with the laws of disease in flesh it will manifest for them in flesh.

Absent treatments is the power to connect with and direct the Cosmic atmospheric currents which make for positive expression of health, and when we have laid hold of this power, we can change at will any vibration of negativeness with which we find ourself or others expressing, and we do it through the power of thought, feeling and revelation.

These higher laws of relationship are only mysterious and strange to those who do not understand; the Hottentot stands in wonder and amazement at the X-ray machine, but the skilled operator turns on its power in spite of this ignorance and disbelief, and it works whether he believes it or not. Just so the skillful operator in Cosmic Therapeutics can generate, control and direct the power of the Cosmic consciousness which he understands, and it brings its results whether the skeptical mind of man accepts or denies.

This power to manipulate nature's finer forces is only hidden from those who do not seek to find; in the moment a soul knows that it is possible to connect through thought and to manipulate through consciousness, it is born into union with the Energy that creates and can say, "Let there be light" over its own world.

We can stand in the great Cosmic Energy and with tools a thousand times finer than the finest X-ray or vibratory machine known to science and project our thought power into regions of an ether so fine, so vibrant, so vital that the very touch of them upon our being fills us with the great pulsing energy of the universe. In just the instant we connect with these currents our old vibratory rates of living are changed and we have passed from death into life; we are healed to stay healed through conscious union with the all-health currents of the Universe.

There are many clumsy operators in any field of science, and there are plenty of them in this new world of Cosmic Therapeutics, but investigation and application give unfoldment and skill, and we will soon pass into such a complete understanding of these higher laws of being that it will be a novelty to find a life unacquainted with them, and everyone will be using Cosmic Therapeutics in some degree.

The fundamental law of absent treatments is the truth of the Oneness of life and intelligence, and the ready response of the Absolute intelligence to the finite mind.

Each life has its own direct line of thought connection with this Universal Energy, and no matter where it stands in its comprehension, it can be taught to understand this simple truth of thought relationship.

We can think ourselves to the outermost rim of things and there connect with the diverse differentiated energy which can only make for disease and lack, or we can think ourselves to the very center of the Cosmic heart and find there the "peace that passeth understanding." We find this center and attract its energy through human thoughts of power, love, hope, faith, joy, purity, patience and consciousness of infinite union, and our every action carries with it into the external world a power that manifests for us as health in our body and wealth in our environment.

When we know that all life is universal atmospheric intelligence and that it responds to us from any point we touch it, we need then only to throw ourselves into conscious thought union with everything which we desire; forgetting all the weak negative things we do not desire, and this conscious connection leads us into relation with the energy that must eventually manifest in form.

If we want to heal ourselves we stand with our whole life open to the positive creative Cosmic currents and let them beat through us and around us; we will then and there to pass our whole being into union with every creative universal force, and to feel the power of its energy sweeping through us; we hold our life to this higher understanding until the great flood tide of the universe comes sweeping along our veins and through our being, washing away in its resistless force all the lesser moorings which hold us to the thoughts of disease or decay; we have then the life more abundantly than is promised and we feel that we have entered into that place that is prepared for the people of God; we are healed to stay healed for the very life blood of the universe is in our veins.

If we then want to give an absent treatment, and send to another this Energy that creates we just take the thoughts of our Cosmic atmospheric relationship in our mind, and reaching out first in perfect thinking we build for them a perfect thought body, and place it in the Cosmic Energy; holding fast to this image we pass with it into the deeper states of being where thinking ceases, and knowing is the law, and we bid them stand forth with us in conscious union whole, complete, the God-child, one with the all-health of the Universe.

When we can do this, our work is finished, and we can let them go, secure in the consciousness that they are one with us in strength and power. When we have really understood this higher law of recognition we look with all-seeing eyes into the face of Cosmic Intelligence, and we see the infinite supply answering our finite lack, we abide in a position of knowing which passes us externally into health of body and environment.

How To Give Absent Treatment

Concentrate your mind on the one whom you wish to heal, then build a mental vision of him; see him in consciousness just as whole and perfect as if he was really radiant with health. Make believe that he is standing before you a perfect picture of physical perfection, work on your vision until you can produce and hold the most beautiful idealized picture of human beauty of flesh, form and character. Never forget to illumine your perfect thought-patient with a divine light of spiritual radiance. This perfected "make-believe-self" must be the risen God within them and it must come forth resplendent in a new glory. When you can hold a perfect vision of him and make yourself blind to anything but this image of beauty, health and power--then place him in the Divine Life and leave him. God, the great universal intelligence, will make the balance good. He will finish what you have begun. There is concerted action between the atomic mind of infinite substance and the mind of man, "and as the Father raiseth up the dead and quickeneth them, so has he given the son the power to quicken whom He will."

This vision held daily and intensified by belief and conscious command will be accepted by the spiritual consciousness of the patient and whether his surface mind accept it or not, his deeper consciousness gives the stimulation to his body and this registers it in form and he is healed to stay healed through the silent laws of mind. "And he stood between the living and the dead and the plague was stayed" because by his own transcendent consciousness he set in operation the higher laws of intelligence in substance.

It is written that in the Psychological Institute in France, Professor Prisbram, in one of his psychological experiments, asked a patient to think powerfully and concentratedly upon a make-believe vision of a bottle--he did, with his hand on a sensitive plate in a developing fluid, and slowly the picture of the bottle registered upon the plate.

Just as this make-believe bottle registered upon the plate, just so does the make-believe perfect flesh-body register in the cells of the old, and under the law of renewal of tissue, it is developed into form.

This vision is the true self that is latent in every life. "The first man, Adam, was of the earth, earthy, the last man, Adam, was a living soul." "There is a body terrestrial and there is a body celestial, and the glory of the terrestrial is one and the glory of the celestial is another." And with the vision of the celestial body, in which the consciousness vibrates as a living soul, our treatment is accomplished and we have made our mind a conscious part of the mighty plan and we can ask whatsoever we will and it will be granted.

How often shall we treat an absent patient?

Three times daily and between these times forget them utterly, give them to the Cosmic forces, the Absolute. Holding on to a patient in thought often delays his recovery. When you have done your spiritual visualizing powerfully and perfectly, stop! The Universal Law will do the rest; never give an anxious thought to them, nor recognize death; vibrate life and more and more life to them and just as the current runs along the wire just so this silent Cosmic intelligence will flow from you to them, and health will come, sometimes slowly, sometimes quickly, back along their veins.

9 789359 394374